Learning to preach today

A GUIDE FOR COMMUNICATORS and LISTENERS

Achim Härtner / Holger Eschmann

CLIFF COLLEGE
—PUBLISHING—

ISBN 1 898362 33 5
© 2004 Achim Härtner / Holger Eschmann
in Association with Cliff College Publishing

British Library Cataloguing in Publication Data.
A catalogue record for this book is available
from the British Library.

**Cliff College Publishing,
Calver, Hope Valley, Nr Sheffield S32 3XG**

Printed by:
from data supplied on disk

MOORLEY'S Print & Publishing

23 Park Rd., Ilkeston, Derbys DE7 5DA
Tel/Fax: (0115) 932 0643

CONTENTS

Part B: Practical guide

b) The reception area of the mind
   The search for direction
   Informative discourse
c) The reception area of the will
   The search for a decision
   Challenging discourse

Part C: Consolidation:
The sermon as communication of the gospel

4. The work of the preacher in the light of the Hamburg
   communication model
   a) The content aspect of preaching
   b) The self-disclosure aspect of preaching
   c) The relationship aspect of preaching
   d) The appeal aspect of preaching
   e) Looking back and looking ahead

1. The language of images as the mother tongue of faith
2. Five characteristics of religious symbols
3. Five rules for using symbols in the sermon

Introduction: An encouragement to preach

The purpose of this book is to encourage people to preach. There are various reasons why this is necessary and important. Anyone who preaches will be keenly aware of the fact that preaching is no easy business. From the days of Moses, the prophet Isaiah and John the Baptist, from Martin Luther and John Wesley through Dietrich Bonhoeffer and Martin Luther King Jr. to the present day, preaching has been experienced not solely as a joyful activity, but also as a difficult one. Swiss Protestant theologian Karl Barth (1886-1968) once described the dilemma of Christian preaching in the following words: "As theologians we are supposed to talk about God. We are, however, human beings and, as such, we cannot speak about God. We must know both that we should and that we cannot, and it is precisely this knowledge that will cause us to give the glory to God. This is the difficulty we face; everything else is child's play."[1] A person who preaches will have to stand within this tension but may, at the same time, go forward in confidence, while asking the question, "How do we get to the point, where preaching becomes a joy and where our sermons radiate the calm assurance of faith?"

The motive for encouraging people to preach must be the original motive for preaching *per se*: the voice and testimony of God, which are not at our disposal. As preachers we must therefore first and foremost dedicate ourselves to the study of the scriptures and prayer. We may apply Martin Luther's statement to preaching: "Work on our sermon as if all our praying were of no avail and pray as if all our work were of no avail."[2] The preaching of God's redemptive love for our world is an invitation to believe and embrace the Christian life. It is founded on the covenant promise of God in Jesus Christ, whose word applies also to those who preach today and those who will be preaching tomorrow:

The original motive for preaching

---

1 K. Barth, Das Wort Gottes als Aufgabe der Theologie (1922), in: K.-J. Kuschel (Ed.), Lust an der Erkenntnis: Die Theologie des 20. Jahrhunderts, Munich/Zurich 1986, pp. 93 – 110, citation p. 93.
2 H. Hirschler, Biblisch predigen, 3rd Ed. Hannover 1992, p. 43.

"And surely I am with you always, to the very end of the age." (Matt. 28:20b)[3]

The appropriateness of preaching as a form of discourse in our modern day church services and the community has been widely disputed for some time both within the church and outside it. "All over the country, so much is being done to proclaim the Christian faith! But is it not, with very few exceptions, institutionalised irrelevance?"[4] Those who believe that preaching has a future will ask the question, how, in the light of such statements, can preaching once again be understood as an opportunity for Christian discourse and become an effective vehicle for communicating the faith?

Encouragement to preach In recent times, the encouragement to preach has increasingly been coming from the congregations: people seek and expect a word that will touch them deep inside. A word that interprets the past, addresses the present, and promises a future. People are once again calling for a propagation of the gospel that is biblically founded and, at the same time, relevant to the lives of the hearers. In an age where the pluralism of opinions makes spiritual orientation increasingly difficult, there is a growing demand for basic biblical information, interpretation and teaching that relate to every-day life. Church attendees today need to know, as much as the unchurched, the reason why they should believe the biblical Word and the preaching of that Word. In our opinion, this reason can only be credibly given if preaching is not presented in isolation, but as part of an ongoing process of communicating the gospel (Ernst Lange) which includes the expression of faith, love and hope of the church as a whole.

Learning to preach
This book is aimed primarily at those who want to learn to preach. This includes students of theology, prospective "profess-

---

3 Bible quotations are taken from the Holy Bible New International Version (NIV), © 1973, 1978, 1984 by International Bible Society, Colorado Springs, CO, U.S.A.

4 G. Ebeling, Das Wesen des christlichen Glaubens, Tübingen 1959, p. 9 (transl. K. Schäfer).

ional" preachers who are looking for basic guidelines and practically orientated help to fulfil their role. However, experienced preachers of the Word may too pick up this book, because they want to reassess their preaching and improve certain aspects of it. In particular, we would like to address "non-professional" preachers who, like their full-time counterparts, are "*God's* fellow-workers" (1 Cor. 3:9). In all types of churches, more and more people who do not hold a theology degree are being entrusted with the task of preaching: lay preachers, readers, etc. These are the kind of people that we would like to encourage with our book, whose preaching is not in competition with that of the full-time preaching ministry, but rather serves as a necessary complement to it. In this edition, we also call upon both the preachers and the hearers to take responsibility together for the preaching activity. In that sense, the book is addressed also to those who actively follow the sermon and, feeling a shared responsibility for its content, want to offer an informed response to the preacher. So "Learning to preach" is also a book for people who want to learn to listen to sermons!

Shared responsibility

This short manual of homiletics (the art of preaching) is divided into three main parts: Part A looks at the fundamentals of preaching. In this Part, the purpose and aim, and the opportunities and conditions of preaching are examined. Part B offers practical guidelines for preparing sermons. In five steps, the central issues of practical preaching are discussed, starting from the initial work on the text and the topic through to the congregation's evaluation of the sermon after it has been preached. Exercises and tasks at various points throughout this part enable preachers and hearers to reflect on their own experience in the light of the relevant theoretical descriptions. Finally, Part C provides a series of reinforcing and consolidating thoughts regarding the activity of preaching based on the findings of modern communication studies. In addition, theoretical relations and practical examples of vivid preaching will be presented which are intended to help the readers, both full-time ministers and lay preachers, to develop creativity in the propagation of the gospel.

The text of this book has been written jointly by both of its authors; where the pronoun "I" is used, it refers to both authors. When writing a book that is meant to appeal to men and women alike, this intention must be reflected linguistically. For this reason, both the feminine and masculine pronouns will be used but all such references are only coincidental and the relevance is, of course, inclusive.

Acknowledgements

The content of this book is the result of the preaching experience of its authors in local church ministry and their work in training students in theology and practical ministry at the Theological Seminary of the United Methodist Church in Reutlingen, Germany. Further impulses result from the involvement of both authors in training lay preachers and conducting homiletic seminars for pastors in various countries and contexts. Fruitful discussions of the book's contents outside of the German-speaking part of Europe have given reason and encouragement for an English edition. Konrad Schäfer has translated the German manuscript (including the quotes unless otherwise noted) with both professional diligence and personal commitment. We would also like to thank Cliff College (Sheffield, GB), in particular Rev. Richard Jackson, Postgraduate Tutor, who showed great dedication in publishing this book. We are grateful too for the additional contributions to the cost of translating and publishing made by Reutlingen Theological Seminary, the Foundation for Evangelism (Lake Junaluska, USA), and the Board of Mission of the United Methodist Church in Germany. Finally, we would like to thank all those who have supported this project in various ways, especially our two families who sacrificed many an hour that might have been spent together.

Reutlingen, August 2003
Achim Härtner and Holger Eschmann

Part A: Fundamentals

Chapter 1: Theological clarification regarding present day preaching

Before discussing concrete steps to prepare a sermon, we need to ask some fundamental questions in the first chapter of this book: "Why do we preach in the church?", "What are the characteristics of a sermon?", "Can preaching be learnt?", "What are the challenges facing preaching in our present-day society?" These are all questions to which there are no easy and probably no conclusive answers. Many issues will merely be touched upon, as a full academic discussion would go beyond the scope of this book. Nonetheless, we believe it is helpful to begin with such fundamental questions in order to clarify our own preaching and to position it within a larger framework. Many of the topics that are only briefly touched upon in this first chapter will be covered in more depth in subsequent chapters, where examples will also be given.

I. The reason for preaching

An Ethiopian proverb says: "The word that helps you cannot come from your own mouth." This proverb expresses a basic human experience: in life, we depend on other people – particularly in a time of crisis - to help us break out of our "revolving around ourselves", and to give us new perspectives and show us new opportunities. No one can, in the long run, live **Our faith** without the care and the encouragement of others. What this **depends on** proverb says about human existence in general applies especially **someone** to the Christian faith. No one can become or remain a Christian **telling us** by him/herself. Our faith depends on someone telling us of the **of the good** good news of God and His people - in other words, on someone **news of** preaching. "Faith comes from hearing the message," the Apostle **God and** Paul wrote in his letter to the church in Rome (Rom. 10:17). **His people** German Protestant reformer Martin Luther translated this passage: "Faith comes from preaching." Here the word preaching, of course, is not limited to the classical Sunday morning sermon in a church service; it includes all forms of proclaiming the good news. God uses human speech and hearing to make His voice heard, to stir up faith and build His church. Therefore preaching is not given to the church to be used as and when the church pleases; rather, the church has been commissioned to preach from the very beginning. That is one side of the coin: God commissions people to propagate the gospel in word and deed. The other side is that people begin of their own accord to talk about that which has liberated them and affects their innermost being. The bible and church history are full of stories where people could not or would not keep their experience of God's love to themselves, but shared it with others. Moved by God's Spirit, they crossed physical and social boundaries to share something of which their hearts were full. To them, spreading the word of the mercy of God and of His coming to His creation is not a burdensome duty, but a heartfelt desire to which they feel compelled.

It is in this tension between gift and responsibility, enthusiasm and commission that our preaching is situated today. As pastors, lay preachers or readers appointed by our churches in the name of the triune God, we are called and commissioned to preach. This can be quite an arduous and agonising experience if one has spent hours over an empty sheet of paper, trying to prepare a sermon but lacking any convincing ideas. However, we endure this only because we ourselves, long before having been appointed by our respective churches, have been touched by the Word of God and feel compelled to share something of the gift of the love of Jesus Christ with others. For this reason, preaching is primarily a matter **Preaching is** of joy and enthusiasm: "Preaching is enjoyable, it is a *delight.* **enjoyable, it** This is the first thing that needs to be taught in a manual on **is a delight** preaching. Point one of paragraph one states: Teaching to preach is teaching to enjoy; preaching should lead to joy! It is in joy that speaking about God fulfils its purpose."[5]

---

5   R. Bohren, Predigtlehre, 4th Ed., Munich 1980, p. 17.

14

II. The characteristics of preaching

So what is a sermon? It is a propagation of the gospel, as we **What is a** have already pointed out in the previous paragraphs. We must, **sermon?** however, distinguish between this broad meaning of the term, and a more specific type of preaching, namely the sermon in a Christian church service. The primary aim of this book is to provide help for this specific instance of preaching, although much of what will be discussed may also be applied to other forms of preaching the gospel.

1. A DEFINITION

The following classical definition is intended to help initially identify what characterises a Sunday church sermon:

> "The sermon is a form of speech which must focus entirely on the present, but in which the Christian faith, the 'old' gospel, must speak, within the horizon of the modern-day consciousness, to both the Christian church and society as a whole."[6]

What does that mean?

2. THE SERMON AS A SPEECH

In this definition, it is said that a sermon is a speech, thus emphasising its oral nature. There is a difference between reading bible verses, a theological essay or a book about preaching or being addressed by a preacher in a church service. I am usually much more open when being addressed directly and orally. I cannot close my ears as I can my eyes. On the other hand, however, I cannot read the sentences I have heard over again as I can when reading a book, or look up any words that I may not have understood. Due to the sermon's oral nature, rhetorical issues such as structure and organisation, language and form used, and presentation are important. These issues will be covered later in more depth.

---

6   W. Trillhaas, Einführung in die Predigtlehre, 3rd Ed., Darmstadt 1983, p. IX.

3. THE CONTENT

The content of the sermon is determined by Jesus Christ

Something else that is said in the above definition is that the content of the sermon is determined by the gospel of Jesus Christ. This is essentially the criterion that distinguishes a sermon from other speeches. A speech can be structured to perfection and presented in the best possible way; but it can only be called a sermon if it tells the good news of God and man. For this reason the Christian sermon must "remain focused on its subject and [must not] want to compete in fields that have not been entrusted to it for cultivation. The hearers must be able to rest assured that they will hear in the sermon that which they are in need of, which they cannot be told elsewhere in this particular form."[7] Now, this qualification is not a restriction, because the terms "Christian faith" and "gospel" as definitions of the sermon content are wide. They provide the basis and the scope for the Christian sermon without specifying the concrete individual topic. There are essentially two ways in which the preacher can arrive at a specific topic: either he interprets a given passage of scripture or he deals with a fundamental aspect of the Christian faith and relates it to the situation of the hearers. He may also start with the situation, the circumstances in which the preachers or hearers find themselves, and relate these to statements of Christian tradition. These two approaches are not mutually exclusive. In a context where biblical texts do not have automatic relevance to the hearers (any more), as in the case of evangelistic events, it may be appropriate to start with their circumstances and move from there to the biblical message. This reduces the danger of preaching above people's heads. On the other hand, there is a strong case - particularly in a church service - for beginning a sermon with a passage of scripture. The diversity of scripture helps to prevent monotony which may result from sermons being based for the most part on a given situation. Moreover, the biblical texts have a dynamic and proper motion that can inspire the preacher and the hearers and generate faith.

---

7   H. M. Müller, Homiletik, Berlin/New York 1995, p. 204.

4. THE SITUATION OF THE SERMON

The third important characteristic mentioned in our definition is that the sermon must focus on the present and take place within the horizon of the modern-day consciousness as it has been shaped by the political, social and cultural development. This fact has already been addressed in the previous paragraph. A sermon is more than a preservation and constant reiteration of pre-formulated doctrines of faith and more than mere recitation of scripture. A sermon must translate a message which was given at a different time to a different culture, making it relevant to the here and now. A Christian speech can only be called a sermon if it is directed specifically towards its audience. A clear understanding of the addressees and their circumstances may be gained with the help of the theologian Ernst Lange's distinction between the "general homiletic situation" and the specific "local situation". "The 'general homiletic situation' includes the macrocosm of the societal order and public life with its constant rapid changes, political events and ideas and, above all, their effects on the people: hopes, fears, resignation, the feeling of impotence in respect of societal developments. The general homiletic situation comprises all those factors that must be accepted more or less as given at a particular time."[8] The preacher learns about the general homiletic situation first and foremost from the mass media, from studies and surveys regarding social issues, and from contemporary art which expresses present-day sentiments. The church calendar should also be considered within the context of the general homiletic situation. The "local situation", in contrast, comprises "those events, relations, conflicts, sentiments, judgements and the prejudice that the preacher does not learn about from the newspapers, as they are relevant alone to the local community and congregation; these factors can only be determined through the preacher's own investigations or from sharing with members of the congregation and from discussions with other church workers, and can be influenced, resolved and changed through the sermon, because they belong to the

The sermon focuses on the present

The general homiletic situation

The local situation

---

8   E. Lange, Predigen als Beruf, 2nd Ed., Munich 1987, p. 38.

immediate area of responsibility of the preacher and the church."[9] In addition to these two ways of understanding the circumstances of the hearers of the sermon there is a third way which does not result from direct observation. The preacher must perceive his 'opposite' (and him/herself!) from the perspective of the Christian faith, as a person upon whom God has laid his hand, a person whom God has created and reconciled to himself, with whom she walks and for whom she has a destiny. Without this theological perspective the hearers of the sermon would not be adequately included.

5. THE PREACHING COMMUNITY AND THE GENERAL PUBLIC

Finally, the above definition of a sermon states that the gospel should be proclaimed to society as a whole as well as the Christian church. If the Christian church is the addressee of the sermon the propagation of the gospel is directed not at an individual - as it is in Christian counselling - but at the community of the seekers and the believers. Although it has proved useful in practice for the preacher to imagine one or at least only a few potential hearers during preparation so as to ensure that the sermon has a clear focus, it must be remembered that preaching in a church service is directed at the congregation as a whole. The sermon speaks to people who have been brought into fellowship and equipped with various gifts for the benefit of one another. Within this community, there is a mutual giving and receiving, a sharing of joy and grief of which the preaching is a part. Of course, the spiritual gifting of the church congregation and the fellowship between the congregation and the preacher are very often not immediately noticeable. It is therefore necessary - despite and in **The sermon** the midst of all the shortcomings of the church as we know it - **addresses the** continually to recognise these factors in both senses of the word: **church and** to identify them and to appreciate and utilise them. Where this **society** happens, the preacher will find helpful words for the church and, vice versa, she will receive the support of the congregation. The

9   Loc. cit., p. 38 f.

18

fact that the sermon addresses society as a whole as well as the church means that the preaching may be directed at the outside as well as the inside. This does not only apply to preaching at evangelistic events, but also to preaching in a church service. The sermon is concerned not only with internal church affairs; it is public by nature and therefore there is and must be room for public concerns. It occurs within a public context. Preaching is, like all the actions of the Christian church, characterised theologically by the interdependence of gathering and sending.[10] In the sermon, edifying, evangelistic, caring and political impulses are closely intertwined. The public nature of preaching is evident from the root of the verb itself: to preach comes from the Latin verb *praedicare* which means to speak publicly and proclaim.

6. THE PREACHER AS AN INDIVIDUAL

There remains one element of preaching that is not emphasised enough in the definition we have used. If one considers the conditions surrounding a sermon one must also mention the individual who preaches it. It is only through the person of the preacher that the biblical-Christian content becomes a sermon. An **Preaching** individual who preaches must perform the task of a translator. For **is** this reason, preaching has been compared with translating or **translating** interpreting: "The preacher seeks to receive the things that touch and affect the hearer into his own person and then to relate his text to these things. In other words: the preacher seeks to process in himself that which his text wants to convey and to present it to the hearers as concerning them, so as to prompt them to a response of their own. What the preacher is doing here can be ... compared to the work of an interpreter. Just as an interpreter mediates between two parties in a conversation, thus enabling them to understand each other, the preacher should facilitate a dialogue between the hearers and the testimony of scripture."[11] To be able to mediate in

---

10 The order in which the terms gathering and sending occur here is not to be interpreted in a chronological sense (first the gathering, then the sending) but in a complementary sense (occurring simultaneously, and complementing and sustaining each other).
11 H. M. Müller, Homiletik, loc. cit., p. 201.

this way, the preacher needs to have a good understanding of both the bible and the situation of the hearers. In this process of interpreting, the sermons of theologians will differ from those of lay preachers as their understanding of the biblical message and of the hearers' situation differs. While theologians will rely - in their sermons - to a large extent on their theological competence, the gifting of lay preachers lies especially in their ability, as experts of everyday life, to relate their experiences of society in general and in the church.

Are there any other characteristics that preachers must possess or requirements they must meet in order to fulfil their ministry? What is it that gives them their legitimacy? Different traditions have different answers to this question. From a Protestant perspective, the doctrine of the priesthood of all believers means that the commission to preach the gospel is given to every Christian. However, in order to ensure the soundness of the sermon content and judge the suitability of the individual for public proclamation of the gospel, the Protestant tradition too has developed the office of the appointed preacher. This office is to a certain extent the opposite to the congregation. This does not, however, make a person who occupies it, in any theological or religious sense, more important. The calling of an individual to the office of a preacher - be it in full-time service of the church or as a lay preacher - involves two main dimensions, which are ultimately interrelated. Firstly, there is the calling by the church. This public calling which normally requires some form of training or academic study involves various recommendation procedures and the public appointment to preach by the respective church organisation. This appointment by the church is based on the New Testament principle that the Christian church calls and commissions an individual to preach. It is ultimately the church that has the competence to judge a person's beliefs regarding Christian doctrine and attitudes to life.[12] The second requirement

The priesthood of all believers

Called to preach

---

12 Cf. M. Luther, That a Christian Assembly has the Right and Power to Judge all Teaching and to Call, Appoint and Dismiss teachers, Established and Proven by Scripture WA 11, pp. 408-416.

for the preaching ministry is a personal conviction that one has **Personal** been called to this ministry by God. This conviction provides the **conviction** motivation and enthusiasm required for the joyous and difficult task of preaching. In contrast to the public appointment, this calling of God has no set form; it may vary considerably, depending on the individual's biography and spiritual growth. It will also always remain an "uncertain conviction", as the Christian's faith is tried. Both these dimensions of the calling to **Confirmation** the preaching ministry are equally important and interrelated. In **by the** situations where one may doubt one's own gifting it is helpful to **church** know that the calling and the commission to preach do not rest solely on oneself as an individual. On the other hand, preaching can degenerate into a tedious duty and routine if one is not continuously driven to share the message by the joy of knowing God's love.

In addition to this basic ecclesiastical and personal calling, one may also expect of the preacher that they are as credible a witness **Credibility** of the gospel as possible. What may sound like an unattainable ideal here can be stated more precisely and circumscribed by the terms "effort of the heart and of the conscience": "Effort of the heart" means a sincere and persistent endeavour to empathise with the people to whom one speaks. The effort "of the conscience" means having the honesty never to say more than one would say to oneself."[13]

7. THE HOMILETIC TRIANGLE

In summary, it can be said that learning to preach involves three main factors. Firstly, there is the biblical Christian tradition, the text or the topic on which the sermon is based and which must be translated into the present. Secondly, in this interpreting process, the hearers and their horizons must be considered in order for the sermon truly to reach and touch the hearts of its audience. Finally, one must consider the preachers and the way they perceive themselves so they can understand their part in the preaching-interpreting process and learn to carry it out in an

---

13 H. M. Müller, Homiletik, loc. cit. p. 198.

21

adequate fashion. These three factors have been described as the homiletic triangle, because they must be viewed not in isolation but rather as reciprocally affecting one another.

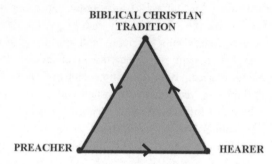

BIBLICAL CHRISTIAN
TRADITION

PREACHER   HEARER

III. The three places of origin of a sermon

Preaching is a process. The preachers and hearers take a journey together with the text or topic. Corresponding to the static illustration of the homiletic triangle, there are three more dynamic factors, the three stages of a journey during which the church sermon develops. The words desk, pulpit and pew may represent these stages, work phases or successive homiletic places.

1. THE DESK

The first place, the desk, stands first and foremost for the groundwork, meditating and unravelling the biblical passage, reflecting on the hearers and the actual organisation of the sermon. This first preparation phase may, in turn, be divided into three steps.

Observing and gathering   a) There is first of all the step of perceiving, observing and gathering. This step is about perceiving and registering the situation of the hearers and one's own situation. The perception phase begins with one's personal study of the text (or topic) during which ideas and thoughts are written down without being evaluated. This is followed by a study of the text with commentaries and other aids and by reflecting on the hearers whom one expects to be present. All this takes place not only at the desk, but also during conversations with church members, while reading the newspaper or even going for a walk.

b) This step of observing and gathering impressions and **Evaluating** information is usually followed by a phase of concentration, **and** comprehension, evaluation and collation of ideas. The per- **collating** ceptions of the text, the topic or the situation from the previous **ideas** step are related, weighed and interpreted. The sermon content is assigned to more general themes of Christian doctrine (e.g. creation, redemption, the church) and contemplated in a more general sense. The previous effects of the text or topic are considered: What results has this topic produced in the past (in church history) and what preconceptions are my hearers likely to have? During this phase of the preparation stage, one has to ask oneself the question, what do I want to achieve with the sermon? This goal should be formulated as clearly as possible before the sermon is written out, so as to ensure that a clear line of thought is recognisable.

c) The third step of the "desk stage" may be described as the **Production** production and formulating phase. In this phase, the sermon is **and** verbalised and given a literary form, in the truest sense of the **formulation** word, that will appeal to the hearers. During this phase, the focus is on the language of preaching, the images and symbols used and the organisation of the sermon. The preacher should also take time to subject his/her sermon once more to a thorough examination with the help of a checklist. As a result, sentences which are too long and therefore not hearer-friendly may be shortened or any incoherence in the use of images rectified.

What may sound like an easy and smooth process in the description of these phases is, in reality, usually connected with severe birth pains. While preparing the sermon, the preacher may **Preaching** experience times of frustration where s/he almost gets to the point **crises** of despair. Research into creative writing has shown that such preaching crises can hardly be avoided. "Not many good sermons have been produced without persistence and earnest seeking ... Blockages and endurance in overcoming them are the *conditio sine qua non* for finding creative solutions. Frustration is the price that must be paid for an idea."[14] The joy over a fruitful sermon and the positive reactions of the hearers will always compensate for the frustration experienced during preparation.

2. THE PULPIT

Sermon delivery

The place or stage of the pulpit represents the presentation of the sermon, its delivery. This homiletic element is often underestimated with the result that the sermon is delivered in a monotonous and unimaginative fashion. However, the somewhat flowery sounding words of the theologian August Tholuck (1799-1877) still apply: "The sermon must be an act of the preacher in his study room, it must again be an act in the pulpit and, descending from the pulpit, he must experience motherly joy, the joy of a mother who has just given birth to a child under the hand of God. It is only when the sermon has been a twofold act of the preacher that it can also be an act in the hearer." When preparing to deliver the sermon, the possibility of contact and communication with the hearers play a role, as do issues regarding manner and presentation, facial expression and gestures, the use of technical aids and - as the sermon is delivered within the context of a church service - the "liturgical presence." (Thomas Kabel). This aspect will be covered in Chapter 5. For now, here is some general advice that Karl Barth gave to his friend and fellow-worker Charlotte von Kirschbaum before one of her first presentations: "Be completely with the subject from which you are proceeding and completely with the hearers, whom you want to reach! Let the speech be born on the way from there to here ... Do not be afraid! Forget yourself and remember that it will surely go well!"[15] Such a conscious forgetting of oneself dispels any fears and tensions. It conveys the message in a convincing way and makes the hearers feel that they are being taken seriously.

---

14 H. Arens/F. Richardt/J. Schulte, Kreativität und Predigtarbeit, 3rd Ed., Munich 1977, p. 30. The Latin expression means: a condition, without which something is not possible.
15 Cited in E. Busch, Karl Barths Lebenslauf, 3rd Ed., Munich 1978, p. 377.

24

3. THE PEW

The third place where the sermon develops is the church pew. It points to the fact that the hearers too are involved in the preaching process. They are involved in deciding, be it consciously or subconsciously, what is heard and what is missed, what is received and what is rejected of that which is said. They influence the way the sermon is processed from the initial acoustic reception right through to putting into practice what they have heard. It may therefore be said that, in the end, there are as many sermons as there are hearers. This does not mean that what the preacher says and how s/he says it is irrelevant, because the hearers anyhow make of the sermon what they want. The principle remains: the one who preaches must ensure with all diligence that the biblical text or the topic of the sermon is properly interpreted and presented to the hearers in a way that they can understand it. Conscientious preparation will preclude confusion. Nonetheless, the pew as a place of birth for a sermon shows that preachers must be aware of the fact that their sermons are heard, received and put into practice in different ways. Indeed, they should encourage this creativity on the part of the hearers by offering them links "which enable them to transpose the message to their own respective situations and to transform it according to their own specific needs."[16] Where a preacher prevents the hearers from participating creatively through a banal one-track message or an authoritarian style, he may jeopardise any congregational response for which he may have hoped.

The hearers' involvement

The working of the Spirit of God has been promised for each of the three places or stages mentioned above. The Spirit gives the preacher ideas while they contemplate the words of the bible, the Spirit takes what the preacher says and makes it alive to the hearers, and the Spirit guides the hearers in the process of receiving, transforming and putting into practice the content of the sermon. In this whole process, the Word of God is coming into being. This interrelation in the preaching process of God acting

The working of the Spirit of God

---

16 I. Reuter, Predigt verstehen, Leipzig 2000, p. 205.

and humans speaking, hearing and doing will be discussed in more detail in the following section.

IV. The sermon within the domain of God's Spirit

When God speaks in the sermon to comfort, to exhort to call to repentance and to generate faith the sermon becomes more than just an informing activity. It may be said, theologically, that a sermon creates what it attests. Thus the speaking process is a process of power: "The word in the holy act is filled with holy power."[17] The statement in the preaching definition given at the beginning that the sermon is "a form of speech which must focus **God is the** entirely on the present" should be understood not merely in the **first hearer** temporal sense, but first and foremost in the sense that the Spirit **of the** and the Word of God are present during the preaching process. **sermon** God is the "first hearer" of the sermon.[18] It is God who decides what the preaching is worth and who has the final say after the sermon has finished. Everything depends on the way God's presence is manifested."[19] For the preachers, there are two sides to this statement. On the one hand, it relieves them when it comes to the difficult task of interpreting, because it is the Holy Spirit rather than the human being who has the last say and the Spirit determines the worth or worthlessness of human words. For me this assurance protects against any feeling of resignation, when I notice that something is not coming across the way I meant it to or when I simply cannot find the words to express what is laid on my heart. On the other hand, tremendous claims are made in this statement: if it is ultimately the manifestation of God's presence that decides everything, how can I as the preacher then vouch for his presence, never mind guarantee it? Given these requirements, is it at all possible to learn to preach? After all, God's presence is not at the disposal of us human beings and we cannot administer

---

17 M. Josuttis, Die Einführung in das Leben, Gütersloh 1996, p. 104.
18 "That is why it is a daring thing to preach: for when I ascend to the holy place – whether the church be packed or virtually empty, whether I take note of this or not: I have a hearer beside those that I can see, an invisible hearer, God in Heaven, whom I can of course not see, yet he can see me." S. Kierkegaard, Einübung ins Christentum (1850), Gesammelte Werke, Vol. 26, p. 226.

his grace. Now, a book entitled "Learning to preach" would probably not have been written if its authors were not convinced that there was something that could be learned with regard to preaching. However, one must take care to distinguish between that which lies within the sphere of the human and that which would go beyond the limits of human ability and may therefore be left to God. The faith of the hearers (and the preachers!) cannot be generated by the human if it is truly the Christian faith. It is God himself who gives faith to us humans through preaching so that we, in turn, can put our trust in God. This frees the preacher from any unrealistic aspirations to be successful. On the other hand, it does not mean that they are relieved from the responsibility of working on the sermon. In the course of this book, we will see that there are things the preacher can do to ensure that the message preached is factually and doctrinally as accurate as possible and as relevant to the situation as possible, that it does not go above the heads of the hearers, but is delivered in a comprehensible and sensitive manner.

If we understand preaching as God's Word and human words or - more precisely - as God's Word in the form of human words, the spiritual dimension gains in importance. Preparing a sermon still means to diligently study a biblical text or conscientiously reflect on a Christian theme in order to obtain a message for the sermon. It still involves the study of psychological and societal factors in order to reach the hearers as directly as possible in the world in which they live. In all this, however, the spiritual foundation of these endeavours must be considered. "Practical pastoral work necessitates a spiritual basis ... Every religious act requires spiritual preparation."[20] The power to perform a spiritual task such as preaching can only be obtained on the basis of a spiritual existence. For this reason, prayer plays a vital role in the preparation of a sermon. Yet here too we must be careful: it is not human ability versus the miraculous. The Spirit of God must not be an excuse for laziness. The practical theologian Rudolf Bohren

God's Word and humans words

The role of prayer

---

19   R. Bohren, Predigtlehre, 4th Ed., Munich 1980, p. 454.
20   M. Josuttis, Die Einführung in das Leben, loc. cit., p. 48f.

27

introduced the term "theonomous reciprocity" in this context. This term means that, during the preaching process, the Holy Spirit brings what the human does into his service: "Miracles and technology are ... not opposed to one another; they merely indicate different aspects of the theonomous reciprocity. When the Spirit of God works in us, with us and through us, I speak of a miracle. Where we, however, are put to work by the Spirit of God and, consequently, get down to work ourselves, methods are involved, technology is applied, art is performed and science is employed. In the partnership with the Holy Spirit, methods, art, technology, science are not excluded, even if they enter into the $\kappa\rho\iota\sigma\iota\varsigma$ (krisis) of the Spirit."[21]

V. The language of preaching and types of sermons

Closely related to the above is the consideration whether there is a particular language of preaching which is particularly suited to the character of God's Word in the form of human words. On this question, the American teacher of homiletics Richard Lischer distinguishes between form and language. According to him, no particular norms have been laid down in respect of the form of sermon, either in the scriptures or in church history. "The Holy Spirit uses all forms, but is not tied to any" (Richard Lischer). The good news of God redeeming his world can be propagated by lay people and ordained ministers alike, by women or men, by the educated or by the uneducated, whereby each group has its own particular gifting and emphasis. It can be told in an evangelistic, faith generating way or, to the church, in a comforting or socio-

Promise politically challenging way. However, Lischer stresses the fact that there is a language, a speech act, with which preaching is inseparably connected, i.e. the promise. For the promise has a personal dimension. It is more than a mere message that can simply be disassociated from the sender and the receiver. It contains the assurance of God's presence. This assurance can be trusted because God's name itself is a promise (I am present! Ex. 3:14 according to Martin Buber's translation) and because His

---

21   R. Bohren, loc. cit., p. 77.

promise forms the basis of his dealings with His people of Jews and Christians throughout history. This kind of promise is realistic, because it gives the assurance of the grace of God, while not denying the separation of man from God through sin. The promise opens up the future without having to flee the present with its fragmentary nature. A sermon, which is based on the speech act of the promise, assures the hearer of the faithfulness of God who is with us. One way this can be done is by addressing the opposite directly. The promise may, however, also be conveyed indirectly, i.e. through stories, parables and pictures, enlightening the hearers and opening up new prospects of hope. Whichever of these forms the preacher decides to use depends largely on the bible passage on which the sermon is based and the situation of the hearers. This subject will be further discussed in chapter 3.

The fact that the sermon is not inextricably tied to a particular form has resulted in different kinds or types of sermons developing in the history of preaching. According to the content, form and occasion of the sermon, one can distinguish between teaching sermons, pastoral sermons, evangelistic sermons, prophetic sermons, dialogue sermons, narrative sermons and case sermons. These sermon types are not fixed categories and they commonly occur as hybrid forms. Nonetheless, it makes sense to distinguish them, as they can help us to identify once more the main characteristics of the sermon, which they each represent in their own particular way.

(1) The *teaching sermon* shows us first and foremost that good rhetoric alone does not make a sermon. There are Christian themes which are fundamental to preaching. Teaching sermons appeal to the minds of the hearers and are characterised by a high density of information. These sermons strengthen the church members in their responsibility to give others the reason for their faith and hope (1 Pet. 3:15).

The teaching sermon

(2) The *pastoral sermon* is a reminder of the fact that God has promised the preacher that the God of all comfort (2 Cor. 1:3f)

The pastoral sermon

29

desires to reveal Himself and let the people experience God's love. The pastoral sermon is more assuring in character than informative or appellative. It conveys a sense of security and comfort and touches the hearers in their innermost being. That is why a pastoral sermon always speaks "about the decisive theme: about God as Lord and the situations relevant to human existence."[22]

The evangelistic sermon
(3) The *evangelistic sermon* brings to our attention the fact that the aim of all preaching is to generate faith and to challenge people to respond to the redeeming love of God. This type of sermon takes the reality of unbelief seriously and tries to give direction to the hearers so they can get to the point of committing their lives to following Jesus Christ. An evangelistic sermon must especially be "an elementary discourse on God and His redemption on behalf of man".[23] The preacher will formulate the sermon in a very personal way to reach their hearers, so that they can respond positively to the message of God's salvation and comprehend it with their whole being.

The prophetic sermon
(4) The *prophetic sermon* emphasises the fact that preaching must be relevant to the present day and challenge the hearers to action. Societal and political controversies, ethical and social issues are addressed from a Christian perspective. As with the evangelistic sermon, the hearers are called to reconsider, to change and to act. The prophetic sermon therefore contains both confrontational and appellative elements.

The dialogue
(5) The *dialogue sermon* reminds us that preaching is not one-way communication nor is it a one-person affair, but, following the principle of the priesthood of all believers, a matter of the church. The term dialogue sermon is not meant here merely to describe the complex type of sermon in which two preachers talk about a text, with or without prior consultation. Rather, it comprises all forms of participation of the church in the preaching

---

22 H. van der Geest, Das Wort geschieht, Zurich 1991, p. 11.
23 W. Klaiber, Call and Response. Biblical Foundations of a Theology of Evangelism, Nashville 1997, p. 203.

process, be it through discussions before or after the sermon, through questions during the service or through a preaching team.

(6) The *narrative sermon* is based on the theological realisation that an abstract way of speaking that contains a large amount of theological terminology alone cannot do justice to the biblical testimony of God. God is "a God on the move, a God who is involved in stories. Talking about this God therefore means making his story heard."[24] The most suitable form of language to tell God's story with his people is the narrative. The term narrative, however, does not imply that this type of preaching can be successful without diligence and thorough preparation.

The narrative sermon

(7) Finally, in the *case sermon*, particular emphasis is placed on the realisation that all preaching of the gospel must give due consideration to the situation of the hearer. As the name tells us, this type of sermon is determined mainly by the case, i.e. the particular circumstances of the people concerned. Case sermons for special events in the lives of church members, such as baptisms, marriages or funerals, will contain elements of the pastoral sermon, but may also take into account particular doctrinal content, which is generally associated with the teaching sermon.

The case sermon

VI. The correlation of the sermon and the church service

With all the preparation, one should not forget that preaching is part of the church service - an important constituent part, but nonetheless only one part. Therefore one should avoid the common notion of the church service as "the frame of the sermon", because it is incorrect. The church service is not merely frame surrounding the sermon. It is itself precious, full of treasured elements and possibilities. What is important is that the sermon is in tune with the service in which it takes place. A clear thread should be recognisable; i.e. scripture readings, hymns, prayers, etc. should relate to one another and to the sermon. In this context, the time of the service within the church calendar should also be considered.

The service is not merely a frame

The liturgy impacts on the preaching

Preparing the worship service is a creative act, like preparing the sermon and therefore takes time. Sloppiness in this area can easily lead to boredom or a feeling of confusion. This will also have an adverse affect on the sermon, for the liturgy impacts on the preaching, as does the room in which the service takes place and the whole atmosphere of the service.

The sermon and the worship service complement each other and need each other. This is evident if we contrast the focus of the liturgy with that of the sermon. While the role of preachers in the sermon involves acting and giving, the worship service offers them salutary relief, as they can, together with the congregation, depend on familiar and given texts and traditions. The liturgical texts provide a larger context for the sermon and may compensate for any one-sidedness. In turn, the sermon can make general statements in the liturgy come to life in the hearts and minds of the hearers. The various elements in worship can play a part in ensuring that the gospel is communicated in the church service in a holistic manner. Rituals, symbols and actions in the service appeal to different layers of the human being than the spoken word. Finally, the liturgy involves the participants in the service to a greater degree and in a different way than the sermon does: while the sermon is a speech directed towards the hearers, the hymns and prayers, both of intercession and thanksgiving, are directed towards God.

VII. Conditions surrounding the sermon today

Preaching throughout history

Anyone studying the eventful history of the church will notice that preaching has changed again and again over the centuries. After what has been said above, this is hardly surprising; after all, one of the important features of preaching is the fact that - as well as orientating itself by the biblical message - it tries to adapt as much as possible to the world of the people it wants to reach. As the sermon must be relevant to the world in the above sense, it seems appropriate at the end of the introductory chapter of a book about preaching to look at how this world may be characterised

---

24   A. Grözinger, Erzählen und Handeln, München 1989, p. 11.

today. The following attempt to analyse some of the social conditions relevant to preaching, positions this publication in a particular place and time. These thoughts have to do for the most part with the "general homiletic situation", which need to be complemented by a relevant "local situation".

1. THE FLOOD OF INFORMATION AND CHANGING
   PERCEPTIONS
   Our age, which is often referred to as the post-modern age, is characterised by increasingly rapid change. We are bombarded so heavily and incessantly with new facts that it becomes difficult for us as individuals to process them. Countless books, magazines and television and the Internet inundate us with information. Our time is clocked into ever-shorter periods; this is reflected in a dramatic way by the rapidly changing sequences of images in television and cinema advertising and the ever-shorter discussion programmes on the radio. One advantage of this abundance of information is the fact that knowledge is becoming accessible to more and more people and, as a result, the power of the experts is decreasing. Many patients, for example, know more about their illnesses from the Internet and the self-help groups represented there than from the doctors treating them. Similarly, the hearers may well be more informed than the preacher. On the other hand, there are limits to our capacity to take in information. "The more we are overwhelmed with information, the more the background, the perceived value and the correlation of facts recede to the point where this flood of information becomes nothing but a hubbub, a meaningless noise in the background."[25] Yet it is not only the quantity of information that has changed; there has also been a change in the nature of information and the way we process it. The flow of information is determined more and more by economic interests and therefore the efficiency and usability of the information, which affects all areas, including religious communication. In this process of judging information by its usefulness, the notions of a deeper meaning, of the dimensions of

The flood of information

---

25 I. Reuter, loc. cit., p. 20.

33

creativity and poetry or the suggestion that things may be more complex than the mass media would have us believe are perceived as a spanner in the works and consequently discarded.

2. CHANGING NORMS AND VALUES

Tearing down of traditions Our (post-) modern society is characterised by a full-scale tearing down of traditions. Values and norms that used to provide stability to the individual or to groups of people are rapidly losing their credibility in the eyes of the general public. There are ever fewer generally accepted principles. "The great stories are falling apart" (Jean-François Lyotard). This means that individuals must determine to an ever-greater extent for themselves which values apply for them. At the same time, however, the sources of tradition which might provide guidance for this self-determination are being destroyed. "The individual drifts in a sea of stories that are no longer binding, himself void of stories and at the same time so much in need of stories."[26] As a result, the individual finds it increasingly difficult to develop a definite, stable identity and to find a clear focal point in life. Due to the abundance of **Patchwork** information and the choice of lifestyles on offer, post-modern **identity** people are led to create a patchwork identity made up of different possible patterns of life and examples, which takes into account the rapid changes in society. The positive side of this is that people in the highly-developed countries today have an abundance of opportunities for self-realisation, that they can make something of their lives - provided they work hard, can assert themselves and have the necessary finances. This increase in opportunities should not be dismissed as something purely negative. However, the disadvantages are evident. Always having to present oneself to others in the best possible way can be exhausting. This phenomenon also affects the area of religion and the Christian faith. Here, too, the great stories are losing their credibility and **Pragmatic** with them the institutions that represent them, in this case the **religion** church. Postmodern people realise their religiosity through a

---

26 A. Grözinger, Geschichtenlos inmitten von Geschichten, in Wege zum Menschen 48 (1996), p. 484.

selection process with the help of their own individual decisions. These decisions are made to a large degree on a cost-benefit basis: which part of religion is important and beneficial for me and capable of enriching my life. Various ideas and forms are combined. A form of religiosity that suits the individual's life is patched together like a rug, and in doing so the individual no longer draws exclusively from Christian traditions. "The mere fact that someone regularly attends church on a Sunday morning does not mean that he does not go home to read a book about music, dance and religious forms of Sufism or listens to a radio programme on ancient Celtic mythology. The shelves of the bookstores are filled with everything that might interest the religiously curious, carefully sorted in alphabetical order. Those interested can pick from a wide range of crash courses and workshops to learn various forms of meditation and spiritual metamorphosis."[27]

3. INDIVIDUALISATION AND SOCIAL ALIENATION

More choice and the breakdown of established traditions lead to an individualisation of our respective worlds. Things in my life might have been completely different to what they are now: I might for example be living together with a different person, have a different job and go to a different church. This means that today less can be taken for granted than ever before and more is left to me to decide. "Predetermined 'normal' biographies are changing into arbitrary biographies with all the pressures and expectations entailed. The decisive thing about this is that individualisation is ambivalent: on the one hand, it liberates us from having our biographies prescribed to us while, on the other hand, it forces us to construct a biography for ourselves."[28] It is clear that this individualisation of our individual worlds also affects our relationships with one another, causing our society to become **Frag-** increasingly fragmented. A whole range of sub-cultures and **mentation of** scenes are emerging according to age group, occupation, leisure **society**

27 Jede/r ein Sonderfall? Religion in der Schweiz, ed. by A. Dubach and R. Campiche, Basel 1993, p. 306f.
28 A. Grözinger, Differenz-Erfahrung, Waltrop 1994, p. 12.

activities and, most of all, interests and situations at a particular time in life. People with similar interests get together for a limited period (Opera enthusiasts, football fans, PC-freaks, etc.). As a result, our society is developing into a "society of strangers" (Claus Leggewie) which is no longer held together by common traditions and in which the cultural and individual peculiarities of the people are making it increasingly difficult to understand others and empathise with them.

Of course the situation in our society today is far more complex than it has been portrayed in these three descriptions. They do, however, show that the observations and interpretations regarding social issues affect the process of preaching and listening to preaching. How can our preaching today adapt to these issues? Although it is not possible in this context to give conclusive answers, I would like to give some direction at the end of this first part of the book, which I believe will be helpful.

4. A CULTURE OF LIFE INSTEAD OF A FUN CULTURE

Positive alternatives The societal changes described above cannot be dealt with by means of moralistic criticism. Lamenting that everything is so much worse today than it was neither attracts others nor does it present them with alternative ways of life. Withdrawing into a form of Christian fundamentalism, which is suspicious of anything unknown and different and derives its energy primarily from focusing on who it regards as its enemies, is not a solution. Instead, positive alternatives based on the gospel must be offered where social factors threaten to destroy lives. Christians can offer a "culture of life" as an alternative to the consumer culture of our day. In the present context this means that, in the face of the flood of information and the ever-increasing variety of ideas and concepts on offer, less may in fact be more. Our focus must be on quality rather than quantity and we must strive for more depth rather than more choice in order to add meaning to our lives. What we need today is a slowing down of the tempo of our lives - also in respect of our faith - in order for our minds and souls to have time, in order for our superficial experiences to become profound ones. Under these circumstances, preaching in the church service must open up a space where there is time to reflect, where there is room for creativity and poetry, where economic factors are not coming to the fore, but where the people are led to perceive the reality of God in a profound way.

5. "AB INITIO PREACHING" AND THE RELIEF OF THE PREACHER

Based on the analysis of the present situation of our society with the breakdown of traditions and the increasing individualisation, the theologian Albrecht Grözinger arrives at the following conclusion in respect of preaching: "We can no longer depend on the hearers accepting certain concepts as given and plausible when they come to church. We must therefore begin with the elementary things when we preach, that is to say at the **Preaching** beginning. It must be possible to understand the sermon without **must be** any prior knowledge. Our preaching must be plausible in itself; **plausible** we can no longer assume anything as being plausible. We must, **in itself** so to speak, work towards the desired consent from zero."[29] Grözinger refers to this kind of preaching as *ab initio*. The most suitable form of language for *ab initio* preaching is the narrative form. A good story is self-explanatory and plausible in itself. It does not impose anything on the hearers and yet manages to capture their attention. As mentioned before, the content of such story-telling in Christian preaching must, of course, be in accordance with the story of the promises of the triune God towards his world.

In the face of the pressure we experience today as a result of having to construct our biographies and present ourselves **The message** constantly in the most favourable way possible, the message of **of** justification through God alone by grace and faith is very relevant **justification** for our time. It helps us to acknowledge our finiteness and our limitations, to live with them, and to utilise the space we have

---

29   A. Grözinger, "Mit dem Anfang anfangen. Anfängliches Predigen in einer Gesellschaft des Multikulturalismus", in: Predigen aus Leidenschaft, Karlsruhe 1996, pp. 61-78, p. 66.

creatively. The assurance of the love of God and consequently the dignity of man makes it possible to distinguish between that which we humans have been commissioned to do and that which would go far beyond what we are able to do. This assurance protects us from the presumptuous urge to ultimately define our own selves and helps us to remain human and consequently to treat others as humans.

6. MODELS AND COMMUNITY

From the normal biography to the arbitrary biography Due to the change from a normal biography to an arbitrary biography described above, there is a need for models and criteria which help to show what Christian living can mean today. This process of orientation can be initiated and developed through preaching. Preaching is able to create models for Christian living without having to offer finished solutions. It can, however, do more than that. If the dynamics and proper motion of the biblical texts are brought to bear, if the sermon not only informs, but promises and, consequently, imparts grace and life, then sources of strength are opened up to the hearers that make it possible for them to actually live a life as followers of Christ. A process is initiated and sustained in the hearers, which theological tradition

Sanctification calls sanctification. In order to avoid excessive demands on the hearers in this regard, the sermon must stress the fact that sanctification, like justification, is God's doing, which nonetheless involves the human, body and soul. This sanctification has both a personal and a communal dimension. The sanctification "of our

Where preaching produces faith, it also produces love for fellow human beings personal lives involves giving all that pertains to our lives into God's hands and allowing him to shape it. This applies equally to talents in the arts and sciences and to disabilities and burdens with which we have to live."[30] As well as this personal aspect, there is also a communal aspect to sanctification. It is characteristic of the working of the Holy Spirit that, by connecting people with God, the Spirit also connects them with each other. Where preaching produces faith, it also produces love for one's fellow human beings and practical action on their behalf. This is particularly

---

30   W. Klaiber/M. Marquardt, Living Grace. An Outline of United Methodist Theology, Nashville 2001, pp. 297f.

38

important in a society where we no longer know the people around us. Although it is necessary in this context to distinguish between the way we act towards people within the church and in society as a whole, we cannot confine Christian love to the church. The New Testament scriptures are full of accounts in which cultural and social boundaries are crossed. It is time to rediscover this power of preaching that crosses boundaries and produces fellowship.

Part B: Practical guide

Chapter 2: From the preacher's workshop

Preparing a sermon is, to a certain extent, also a craft involving **Preaching** practical skills. Certain things must be learnt. In this chapter, we **is a craft** will discuss how a sermon can be produced according to a set plan. With the help of examples, we will show two different routes for preparing a sermon: a) how the preacher gets from the biblical text to the sermon and b) how they communicate the message beginning from a topic. The sermon preparation process described here does not only take place in the study where the preacher opens up their bible, reads the passage of scripture, meditates on the words of the bible in prayer, gathers thoughts for the sermon, develops and consolidates these thoughts and contemplates, what they want to communicate to their hearers. Any person who preaches regularly will constantly be working on a sermon, be it consciously or subconsciously. The preacher finds and collates material when visiting members, during random conversations, while reading the newspaper. They search - again consciously or subconsciously - for solutions to problems which seem insurmountable. Many preachers will wake up at night after receiving an enlightening thought that can serve as the basis of a sermon. Thus, preachers find themselves in a similar situation to artists, needing creative inspiration. The preacher is dependent on the creative Spirit and must therefore constantly remain open to the Spirit. What is important is that the preacher takes time with the sermon and does not try to finish it in one go. It is advisable to spread the different steps of sermon preparation over several days of the week or, if there is sufficient time, even several weeks.

I. The first route: from the text to the sermon

In most cases, sermon preparation begins with the selection and study of a biblical text. Further steps that I must take in order to arrive at a sermon that will speak to the hearers follow this. I will not always do all that is suggested below. I will often skip one or more stages and sometimes I will spend more time at a particular point, because I encounter more problems than in the following description. It is like in many board games: sometimes the figure will advance swiftly and reach the finishing mark quickly. At other times, however, the player has to go back some spaces and struggles to get home.

Sermon preparation focuses on the Bible and the hearers
In the following, I will suggest steps that may be taken when proceeding from the biblical text to the sermon. In doing so, I will include, from the very beginning, the consideration given to the situation of the hearers. I do this in order to show more clearly the strangeness of biblical texts and their reception or rejection in a given hearer situation. I embark on the journey from the text to the sermon with the knowledge I have in respect of my hearers. Thus, my preparation focuses on both the bible and the hearers. The steps have purposely been kept brief so that they may be used as an outline for sermon preparation. Throughout this chapter, references are given to other chapters of the book where the respective steps are discussed in more detail.

1. SELECTING A BIBLE PASSAGE

First Step: The Lectionary
There are two basic ways in which a biblical text may be selected. I can either follow the Lectionary (i.e. list of assigned readings) which some churches issue and by which they expect their preachers to abide. These orders stipulate a particular bible passage for each Sunday and holy day of the church calendar year on which the preacher must base their sermon. The advantage of such orders is that I do not have to spend time searching for a passage of scripture myself, that the scriptures are selected to suit the time of year, and that relevant up-to-date literature for sermon preparation is available, often including suggestions regarding the liturgical part of the service which are appropriate for the given biblical text or topic. Another advantage of using a Lectionary is that I do not select only my own favourite scriptures, but instead am forced to contemplate thoughts other than my own. An argument against these lists, on the other hand, is that they constitute a set pattern according to which the biblical passages are continually

repeated at particular intervals. The proposed readings therefore do not always reflect the current issues within the church and society as a **Current** whole. There is a danger that something of the prophetic **issues** dimension of preaching may be lost if the biblical word or topic is never selected by the preacher in view of the particular situation.

2. MY FIRST DIALOGUE WITH THE TEXT
This section of the road to the sermon may be subdivided into **Second step** several individual steps:

(1) When I have found a bible passage on which to base my sermon I consider the following points during my initial contemplation:

- Is the text close to me or far from me? Is it easy or difficult to understand?

- Do I feel comfortable with it or is it strange to me? How does it affect me?

After having written down my initial feelings about the text, I proceed along the following stages:

a) I try to rephrase the text in my own words.

b) In the case of narratives, parables and descriptions of situations, I try to put myself in the position of the persons involved and re-enact the passage (maybe even with others).

c) I contemplate the key words of the text or important words that particularly fascinated or annoyed me. I try to grasp the meaning of these words with the help of various dictionaries. I pay attention to the pictures and symbols that occur in the text.

d) I consult various translations of the passage and try to determine how the translators understood particular words and interpreted pictures.

(2) I describe the text with regard to its

- structure,
- climaxes,
- unclear sections,
- ambiguities.

(3) I try to recall other texts, biblical and non-biblical poems, prayers and stories that I believe have something to do with my bible passage.

(4) I consider the time of my sermon on this passage in respect of the church calendar and remind myself of the theme, hymns and psalms traditionally assigned to that Sunday.

(5) I note down any questions and issues that I intend to explore further during my detailed study and exegesis (interpretation of a biblical text according to theological criteria and methods) of the text.

Third step 3. MY FIRST DIALOGUE WITH THE HEARERS

When I begin talking to the hearers in my mind, I try to take into account both levels, the specific situation and the general homiletic situation (cf. Chap.1). The following questions may help me during this step:

(1) I imagine how my thoughts for my sermon might affect the hearers. For this purpose, I visualise, as far as possible, one or more specific individuals and also the situation of my church as a whole (make-up and spirituality of the congregation, situation of the church in the community).

(2) I try to determine whether the ideas that I have had based on the bible passage fit the situation in which I am to preach.

(3) I establish which of the issues addressed by the text I would like to talk to my hearers about.

(4) I reflect on conversations or bits of conversations and experiences which I have recently had with the hearers, for example during pastoral visits, or with friends acquaintances and neighbours.

(5)   I try to find out what societal events and global developments are currently of concern to my hearers.

(6)   I ask myself what I am really hoping to achieve in my hearers when I convey the message of the biblical text: What is my intention as a preacher of the gospel?

All these questions help me with my initial assessment of the homiletic situation, i.e. contemplate what I assume to be the situation of my hearers, the areas affecting their lives and any questions they may have. This subject will be discussed in more detail in Chapter 3.

4. EXEGETICAL AND THEOLOGICAL VERIFICATION OF MY IDEAS REGARDING THE TEXT

During this step, I must treat the biblical text as my **Fourth step** interlocutor. This means that I talk to my text rather than twist and shape it until it suits me. Consequently, the exegetical and theological verification of my ideas must result in corrections. The following questions may be helpful:

(1)   What was the larger context of the passage at the time and from the perspective of the author?

(2)   What goal(s) did the author have in mind and what means (language, style, argumentation, etc.) did she employ to achieve that goal (these goals) in her situation?

(3)   What do commentaries say about the message and the main statements of the text? Are there significant variations or even irreconcilable differences in the interpretations of the text given by the commentaries?

(4)   How does the text fit into the overall testimony of the bible? Does it take up ideas that are frequent throughout the Old and New Testament or does it stand more or less in isolation? What would be missing if this text were not included in the canon of scripture?

(5)   To which main areas of Christian doctrine (e.g. creation, justification, discipleship, the church) does the text belong?

What can I find out in this regard from Bible Dictionaries and other theological literature?

(6) Are there significant differences or similarities between the situations and worldviews of then and now?

The results of this third step are summed up in a few core statements. I then know in what way I must represent the text to the hearers.

5. A LOOK AT PREACHING LITERATURE

Fifth step If I have sermons or meditations in my own library or I am able to obtain good preaching materials elsewhere, I should look at them. With the help of such materials I can find out how others have interpreted the text before me. I will always benefit particularly from the sermons of preachers whom I have learnt to appreciate, from whose sermons I have received something myself. The following steps may be helpful:

(1) I establish what the central idea is by which others have linked the bible passage with their own statements.

(2) I decide which of these ideas appeal to me and which of them I find particularly successful.

(3) I write down which stories, images, examples and illustrations I find convincing.

(4) I consider the effects my text has had in the past (Who has used this text throughout church history and for what purpose?) so I can determine whether I can build on a past message or whether I need to refute it.

While plagiarising is forbidden in an academic context, the following rule applies when gleaning from the sermons of others: plagiarism is the mother of all homiletic inspiration or: in this context, theft is permitted. This means that preachers do not need to state in the sermon from which sources they have obtained their ideas. The hearers are not usually interested.

6. PAUSE FOR INSPIRATION

When I have finished gathering material and checking my **Sixth step** ideas it is best not to begin writing out my sermon, but rather take a break and wait for inspiration. The sermon should be allowed to "grow in the womb" until the inspiring thought is birthed.

Going through this inspiration phase may be arduous, because I am not yet clear about exactly how and what I will be preaching. I don't know whether I will come up with something appropriate. I may experience this phase, also referred to as the frustration phase, as distressing. I have to deal with problems concerning my text and my hearers. How can I build a bridge between the text and the situation to ensure that I am not talking above the heads of the hearers?

The arduousness of this phase is usually offset by the joy over the inspiring thought. Once I have checked whether my idea for the sermon will work, I can deal with the material I have gathered in a purposeful way. I am motivated to preach and therefore able to motivate others to listen. I can name the problem and therefore circumscribe it. I have travelled many difficult roads through trials and errors. Now I am able to offer a solution and put on paper my central thoughts for the sermon.

7. ASSIGNING THE BUILDING BLOCKS

I now assign the insights and impulses gathered in steps 2 to 5 **Seventh step** to the central idea for the sermon and the main thoughts that I have developed. In doing so, I need to have a dual perspective:

(1) Selection: In studying the available material, I must ask myself what is useful in relation to my main thoughts for the sermon and what needs to be omitted. The same applies to any pictures and examples. If something is rejected as unsuitable for this sermon, it does not mean that it cannot be used for other sermons based on the same passage of scripture. It is therefore a good idea to compile a card index or database for sermons where such findings can be sorted and stored according to the relevant texts or topics.

(2) Expansion: During this process, which goes in the exact opposite direction to the point described above, the preacher determines which sections of the sermon need to be expanded and what additional illustrations, symbols or texts may be required. At this point, it may be helpful to take another closer look at the preaching literature.

8. ORGANISATION AND WORDING OF THE SERMON

Eighth step   This step is about drawing up various plans to help me develop my sermon. Next, I venture a first draft of my sermon. The following steps may be helpful:

(1) Based on one or possibly several of the models presented in chapter 4, a plan is drawn up for the organisation of the sermon.

(2) The material from the previous steps is fitted into this plan.

(3) A first provisional wording of the sermon is either written down or spoken unrehearsed on tape. In doing so, I must consider what kind of language is appropriate bearing in mind the three factors of the homiletic triangle (cf. Chapter 1). In other words, I contemplate, whether the language I am using does justice to the biblical text and the sermon content, the hearers, and myself as the preacher with my strengths and weaknesses.

(4) I present this first draft to one individual, say a friend or relative, or a small group of hearers. I invite these people to comment on the sermon and make suggestions.

9. COMPLETING THE MANUSCRIPT AND PLANNING THE SERVICE

Ninth step   The feedback and insights from the conversations regarding the first draft wording of the sermon are recorded and incorporated into the sermon manuscript. Following this, I scrutinise the sermon once more myself with the help of the questions, tips and checklist found in chapter 6. Sufficient time and diligence should also be given to planning the liturgical part of the service to ensure that the congregation experiences the service as an integrated whole rather than a mixture of incoherent elements. In this context, compare the discussion of the relationship between the sermon and the liturgy in chapter 1.

10. THE DELIVERY OF THE SERMON

Tenth step

The final step is to deliver the sermon that I have prepared. In most of the literature on homiletics the delivery of the sermon is given little attention. In this book, a separate chapter has been dedicated to this aspect (Chapter 5).

Example: Preparing a sermon on Matthew 13:10-17

The following example illustrates how a sermon may be produced beginning at the text. Some of the stages described above have been omitted.

My first dialogue with the text

The text

I do not feel comfortable with the text. It appears to me like an "anti-sermon" and I feel like contradicting it. So parables are not intended to give explanations; rather, they constitute a type of discourse intended to veil truths and make them incomprehensible. How can that be so? Didn't Jesus himself tell his disciples stories about peasants and fishermen, women and merchants in order to reveal to them the coming of the kingdom of God? In this passage, however, it says that the parables do not reveal the mysteries of the kingdom of heaven (v.11f), but hide them.

What I find even more annoying is the theory of the "calloused heart" with which Jesus presents us. Is he giving excuses for the failure of his preaching? Why should we as hearers and preachers still try if it is clear from the very beginning who can listen (v.14f)?

What is even more embarrassing is the fact that Jesus goes on to tell his disciples that they are blessed. Does this mean that it is given to a chosen few to understand the mysteries of God? Are they indeed more favoured than even the prophets? Are these words not arrogant and quite "unchristian"(v.16f)?

So I end up in all sorts of contradictions while contemplating this text. Isn't the gospel of Jesus Christ for everyone? How is it then that there are "mysteries" which are inaccessible to most people? Jesus has come to break through all bondage. Here, however, we are told of people who remain bound in their fate. Jesus has gathered to himself a church to which everyone is welcome; but here it is presented as a small group of chosen people.

I note down the following questions for the exegesis:

- How can such contradictions be explained?
- What are the mysteries of the kingdom of heaven?
- What is the relationship between wanting to hear and not being able to hear?
- What is the particular merit of the church that causes Jesus to say that the eyes and ears of the disciples are blessed?

My first dialogue with the hearer

The hearer I will be speaking to students of theology who concern themselves very much with the comprehensibility of a sermon. We have learnt a lot about this aspect in the tutorial: how a sermon can be effectively organised, how it can be prepared in a hearer-friendly way, and how we can offer information in appropriate doses to ensure that we do not overburden the hearers. We have also sought to learn from Jesus how he tells stories and how, through his narration, he involves his audience in God's story with man. We have also gathered a number of observations and experiences of how sermons are received by hearers including ourselves. We have sought to identify where there are blockages, where there is approval, and how a sermon can be understood in a completely different way than intended. Together, we have concluded that a lot can be done to formulate a sermon in a well-structured and comprehensible way.

I presume that not only the students find this text annoying. In many conversations people have told me that they would like sermons that they can understand more easily than the ones they hear in church. They already encounter enough "mysteries" in our theological formulae. A bon mot by Charles H. Spurgeon comes to my mind: "A woman once said, our pastor is like the Good Lord. During the week he's uncertain and on Sundays he's unfathomable." Thus, I can expect a lot of approval if I try to speak in a way that the hearers can understand, if I structure my sermon clearly, and when I give examples that are easy to remember and tell parable-like stories.

Nonetheless, my own sermons have often got very close to being incomprehensible. Even the most fascinating sermon remains ineffective if it does not cause the hearers to develop faith in Jesus. The beautifully paved paths of persuasiveness along which I take my hearers all end at a narrow gate through which they must ultimately pass by themselves.

Is it this awkward truth that the text wants to convey? Does it want to warn me in my hearing and preaching not to put my confidence in that which is attainable and reasonable? Does it want to remind me that the gospel will always remain a word that is opposed to all reason and that its effect cannot be calculated?

I think of people who found their way to Jesus through inarticulate, faltering words, people who were more convinced by a testimony from stammering lips than by rousing speeches. We cannot force people to have a hunger for God's word.

Exegetical and theological verification of the ideas regarding the text

The word "parable" (v.10) must evidently be translated in accordance with the meaning of Hebrew equivalent as "mystery" or "not readily understandable discourse". This term, however, does not refer to the stories that Jesus tells, but to the whole message that he proclaims. This message is so new, so unfamiliar, and so mysterious that it does not fit into the obsolete notions of God. The "mysteries of the kingdom" are evident first and foremost in the person of Jesus Christ and his message about God. A God who demands greater righteousness than that of the keeper of the law (Matt. 5:20) remains incomprehensible to most people. A God who has linked his truth so utterly to the person of his Son

51

(Matt.11:25f) will be rejected by the learned and the wise who have confined him in their theological formulae. So it is all about faith in Jesus as the Christ of God. To those who do not believe in him, even the parables he tells are nothing but strange little tales, not even very logical stories. It is the preacher Jesus alone who vouches for the truth of his preaching.

Now that we have clarified this relationship between God's truth and the person of Jesus we can also understand the statement about the deaf ears and blind eyes better (v.13-15): those who reject the person of Jesus will not see the Kingdom of God, not even from afar. Thus, Jesus' preaching has two mutually exclusive effects. The result is the irreversible order of redemption: man has no way of turning to God of himself; God must first turn towards man, he must open the eyes and ears of man to his redemption. This is why Jesus explicitly makes reference to the passage in Isaiah. It is only with his coming that judgement in all its seriousness and salvation in its full applicability have become clearly evident. God's definite *yes* to us humans must be seen against the background of his definite *no* to our estrangement from him.

However, as the history of God progresses from the *no* to the *yes*, from condemnation to salvation, Jesus calls the disciples blessed, because they see and hear (v.16f). He rejoices over the fact that God's grace is already moving among people. The disciples' faith is not a definite possession; rather, it is constantly being challenged. However, against all appearances and contradictions, God grants them this experience: our sins have been forgiven, peace has come to us, we have obtained life. This love of God is so unmerited, so free, that it is possible for Jesus to speak of the arrival of a new era (v.17). Here, the text refers us back to its beginning. Those who are on Jesus' side, those who discover in him the mystery of God's reign will also see the marks of his kingdom in every-day stories; nature and history thus become the sources of parables.

On the basis of these findings, I arrive at some key theological statements for my sermon: **Key theological statements**

1. Jesus addresses people who have put their trust entirely in him. These people, he says, belong to the new era, for the Kingdom of God is beginning among them.

2. This new era brings to light the characteristics of the former era: unbelief, callousness and hopelessness. They point to the fact that God's grace cannot be earned by man; it is a free gift from God.

3. As long as Jesus speaks, as long as he tells his own story in the parables, it is always possible to take the pathway of trust, there is always hope of forgiveness and salvation. Thus, the invitation to discover with Jesus the marks of the kingdom in our daily lives is extended to us.

These statements are reinforced by the biblical declaration from the theology of Karl Barth: "This is why Jesus speaks in parables ... so that the words spoken by the prophet Isaiah of the ever hearing but never understanding and ever seeing but never perceiving might be fulfilled: the unchangeable order that man does *not* have the possibility of turning to God of himself, but that this possibility is actually *taken away* from man, precisely when God turns him to himself. This order is the mystery of the kingdom, which the disciples of Jesus come to know through him as his disciples and consequently they know in him. Thus, he has drawn them into his loneliness, a loneliness before God and in relation to the whole world."[31]

Pause for inspiration

In this example, we will omit the step of looking at the preaching literature. After taking a break to wait for inspiration I formulate the following central thoughts for the sermon: **Central thoughts for the sermon**

1. Anyone who relies too much on what they can do in preaching will be corrected by the text. This conflict between the

---

31   Kirchliche Dogmatik, Vol. II/2, 3rd Ed., Zurich 1948, p. 495 .

hearers' expectations and the message of the text must come across clearly in the sermon.

2. Anyone who relies too much on the effects of parables and stories is told by the text that it is impossible to bypass the person of Jesus. Like His own life, Jesus' stories always end at the cross and the resurrection. It is from here that they derive their truth and their validity.

3. The comfort of the gospel lies in the fact that Jesus sets little store by what is possible for man and stresses what God can do. This also liberates preachers from the false expectation that they can somehow force the faith of the hearers through their skill and performance.

Assigning the building blocks

Life experience After formulating the central thoughts for the sermon, I assign to them the previously gathered material and search for further impulses to help me to convey to my hearers and myself what I want to share. I find a whole range of different experiences regarding the continually observed inability to allow oneself to be drawn into an exciting story-line or the limitations of anecdotes that I have been told.

1. Fairy tales, such as Little Red Riding Hood, are understood differently by children during different stages in their development. A little child will follow the story in suspense. The scene in the grandmother's house in which Little Red Riding Hood asks the wolf in the grandmother's bed questions and is finally swallowed up has to be told over and over again. In the end, it's all joy, because the grandmother and the child come out of the wolf's belly alive and well. One day, however, the child will make comments like, "But wolves can't speak!" and "If you get eaten by a wolf, aren't you dead and torn into pieces?" What about that? The magic is over. The child is no longer absorbed by the story.

2. The newspapers constantly report incidents where foreigners living in Germany are subjected to abuse and assaulted. Instead of helping the victims, many passers-by close their

eyes and walk away. The victims' and the onlookers' perceptions of this situation are completely different.

Organisation and wording

The *introduction* should make reference to the way the group of students perceive themselves. The hearers are therefore addressed as experts of homiletics who are making good progress in their endeavours to ensure that their preaching of the gospel is comprehensible.

In part 1 of the main section, the uncomfortable statement of the text regarding the purpose of the parables will be discussed. For this discussion, the "anti-sermon" as developed in the first dialogue with the text will be used.

In part 2 of the main section, the opposition of the hearers to this statement will be overcome as they are brought to the realisation that the way of salvation is irreversible. God's *yes* to us in the person of Jesus Christ comes before anything we can do. At this point, the material from the exegetical and theological considerations can be incorporated.

The conclusion will show on the basis of the above realisation that it is not we who generate faith. This is meant as a reassurance to us preachers: despite our preaching skills, which we ought not to hide, we may begin the preparation for our sermons by asking, as the disciples did, "Lord, what shall we do?"

Sermon on Matthew 13:10-17 (R. Heue)
(Weekly service at the Theological Academy of Celle)

Dear fellow students

The matter for discussion here is altogether frustrating. We have spent another entire semester looking at ways to make our sermons more easily understandable. We have checked the density of information, taken the long sentences apart. We have rephrased the difficult theological statements, time and again. We have racked our brains for convincing examples and stories from the everyday lives of our hearers. We have taken to heart what Martin Luther already knew: "... people sleep and cough when we preach the article of justification, but prick up their ears at stories."

And with all this we believe we are following the example of Jesus. Did he not also preach in a way that none of his audience slept or coughed? Did he not capture the everyday experiences of his hearers, the peasants, the fishermen, the merchants, in order to reveal to them the beginning of the kingdom?

Yet now we are supposed to comprehend, in violation of all the principles of homiletics which we so treasure, that the examples and stories, the parables, serve to conceal the mysteries of the kingdom rather than to reveal them.

And that is not all! The fact that Jesus sees the failure of his preaching brings him close to us. But does he have to explain this failure by an entire theory on the callousness of the hearts of his hearers? So the parables are not capable of opening the eyes of most people, because they are not in a position to hear and understand in the first place. If this is true our homiletic skills are in actual fact useless. If most people have not been given a religious antenna there is no point in putting all that effort into sharing the message. The reference to the passage in Isaiah is actually frightening. It says there that people are blind and deaf so that they cannot turn to God and be healed. Does this mean the role of the preacher is merely to help bring about God's judgement? Does this mean the more the preacher speaks to deaf ears, the more the people sleep and cough during the sermon, the more certain they are to perish?

Against this uncomfortable background, it is all the more embarrassing that Jesus commends his disciples, because they see and hear. So a small elite has been chosen to understand the mysteries of God. A few insiders are more fortunate than even the prophets. They see and hear the things that the messengers of the ancient people of God longed to see and hear. Is this then a text meant only for religious elites? A text for the small band of righteous ones? An encouragement for preachers faced with empty pews? Or is it a discourse on the topic: Christians are ordinary people with extraordinary pretensions?!

I believe, dear fellow students, that the best way to understand this attack on our homiletic honour is to discuss it with Jesus. The stories we tell and the examples we give in our sermons often develop their own dynamics. I observe, for example, how a child understands the fairy tale of Little Red Riding Hood. At first, the child follows the narration in suspense. It is absorbed by the story. The dramatic scene in the grandmother's house has to be rehearsed time and again. The terrified little girl questions the wolf, who is lying in the grandmother's bed, about his big eyes and ears and his enormous mouth. Then, all of a sudden, the wolf swallows her up. In the end, it's all joy as the grandmother and Little Red Riding Hood emerge from the wolf's belly alive and well.

One day, however, the suspense is gone. The child begins to comment: But wolves can't speak! Two people in one go? How are they supposed to fit in the wolf's belly? But if you get eaten by a wolf you're dead and all torn up in pieces! With these comments, the magic is over. The fairy tale is no longer suited as a parable; the narrator must think how he can retain his credibility, because the child's distrust of the story begins to reflect on him.

So if Jesus absorbs us into his stories and parables, if he shows us the extraordinary mysteries of the kingdom of heaven he vouches for the credibility of his words with his life and death. The message remains inextricably linked to our trust in Him. Therefore Jesus must reckon that His preaching will remain incomprehensible. Our understanding of the parables reveals which side we are on. To those who reject the narrator, who cannot see the connections between the reality of life and the coming of the kingdom of God through his eyes, the stories of Jesus are merely strange tales which don't even make much sense. A sower, for example, who watches indifferently as three quarters of his seed is lost, who does not take the trouble to put up scarecrows and to remove the stones and weeds from his field will be the object of ridicule, even in a less productive agricultural society. It is only as it becomes clear to the hearers how undeterred, forbearing and infinitely patient God is when it comes to waiting for the good fruit that they are able to trust this story. It is only as I discover Jesus' own fate behind it, how he becomes the seed that is trodden on, dried up and suffocated, how He cannot find root anywhere, how he is finally left with only a grave in the infertile rock, that I can be amazed with him at the unlikely turn of events. So much vanity, so much shame and death, yet in the end so much resurrection and victory, and so many people who find their only comfort in life and death in Him.

So we have found one answer in the fact that the message remains inextricably linked to the one who vouches for it, that with Jesus' stories we are always also told his story. Yet there was more that startled us.

God does not simply fail because people do not trust him. He does not fail, because he is unable to master the complex psychological rules of communication; He himself has blocked the ears and blinded the eyes of the hearers. That is what it says. Yes, it is with Jesus that judgement has come in all its fullness. Those who cannot receive him and the coming of his kingdom do not see salvation in part or from afar; no, they do not see at all. The one message of the cross - two mutually exclusive effects. It is very unlikely that the group of believers in Matthew or any other group in the course of church history would have received these words with a self-righteous or arrogant attitude. Rather, the church throughout the ages has experienced trials, as it learnt that the good message of Jesus Christ met not only with joy, but also with hatred, rejection and persecution.

This is the puzzle which we all have to face, that reality so evidently contradicts the promise, that love so evidently does not prevail. We fail, because there may be conditions, both bad and good, deprivation and cruel suppression of any freedom, dark concrete jungles and luxury apartments in sunny resorts where God's grace simply has no place any more. There, God becomes nothing but paralysis, death and judgement. Our fathers believed that man needed to fear no one as much as God, and their response to this fear was: Go to the cross, go to Jesus, see how the crucified one gathers all the darkness of the world upon his head, how, suffering in our stead, he once and for all expresses our experiences: My God, my God, why have you forsaken me? This is probably where our text ends. It is here that Jesus forestalls the great separation. Here he is counted with the rejected and the unbelievers, there he is the rejected one, so that we may be accepted. This is the direction of the text, from the no to the yes, from the puzzle to the answer.

This is why Jesus finally speaks of joy. He is amazed that God's plan among us humans should come to its fulfilment, despite all the obstacles in communication, despite all our entanglement in guilt and shame. So let God always be God, an illusion, a deceiver, or an accident. Jesus stands before God and on behalf of God saying: Blessed are you!

Let religion always be religion, opium or a dream or dynamite. Jesus is before all religion. And He speaks to us: In my name you will see and hear!

Whether our frustration has turned into joy so quickly does not seem important to me. We find it hard to be rejoicing preachers. What is more important and more appropriate is that we begin the preparation of our sermons where Jesus' disciples always began. They began by asking in consternation: Where is it that we belong, Lord? We are not sure. And how much did the disciples lack! They could no longer pray reciting familiar formulae. Lord, teach us to pray! Right to the very end, they were unsure what they should think of Jesus' way: Lord, where should we go? Their ideas of the world to come were shattered: Lord, will you restore the kingdom of Israel? They lacked the courage to employ their energy, to utilise it as advocates and helpers of the people: Lord, where in this remote place can anyone get enough bread to feed them? Lord, where from? Lord, where to? Lord, with what? Lord, why? So many hard questions, so many embarrassing questions, but questions which received an answer.

This is the assurance that Jesus gives us theologians and preachers. Below mountains of words, time and again, the Word is taking place; from below mountains of questions, suddenly an answer springs to mind.

A personal experience of mine: My own fundamental realisations of faith stem from sermons that I have heard. Tiny fragments here and there, pieces in a mosaic that only came together much later, and yet: Faith came from preaching and theology from faith. This gives me the courage to carry on preaching.

Martin Luther once said: "To preach Christ is a difficult and dangerous thing. If I had known that earlier I would never have preached, but rather said like Moses: Send whom you will. If I did not preach for the sake of the man who died for me, then the world would not be able to pay me enough money." Amen.

II. The second route: from the topic to the sermon

The place Anyone who studies preaching focused not on a biblical text
of the but on a topic will find that the standard textbooks on homiletics
topical say very little about this aspect of preaching. Nonetheless, there is
sermon a place for topical sermons, particularly when preaching to an
audience to whom scriptural references have little or no meaning
at all. People who no longer have knowledge of the bible, do not
accept it as an authority and will consequently not see why they
should believe something, simply because it is written.

When preaching on a biblical text, much emphasis is placed on
diligently interpreting the text. In the case of topical preaching,
however, the analysis of the situation and of the audience and also
a general theological reflection on the topic are of vital
importance. I usually prepare a topical sermon whenever I have
an idea that I consider to be so important that I want to produce a
sermon on it. I extend this idea into a theme which I then seek to
substantiate from a biblical-theological perspective. I will, for
example, preach a topical sermon on the question of hearing
sermons. As with the route from the text to the sermon, the idea,
which springs to my mind suddenly, follows a perception of a
particular problem, the gathering of information on the problem
and a subconscious search for a solution.

1. THE IDEA FOR THE SERMON

First step The sermon preparation begins with a notion, which itself is
already the result of a search. I may be concerned with
discovering what questions are troubling my hearers. If I find
something important in this area I have an idea, which I can then
develop into a topic for a sermon. What my hearers are troubled
with may also be a problem of my own, such as particular issues
related to education or current affairs. I feel pressed to say
something on the issues that are occupying my mind and the minds
of other members of my congregation. That is my topic. I do not
find it in the bible, but in the world in which I live, as a result of
prolonged observations, personal experiences, conversations,
stories, news items, and films.

2. THEOLOGICAL QUESTIONS

I have to justify my idea theologically. For this purpose, I have to consider the following points: **Second step**

(1) The idea must be backed by one or several biblical texts. These texts ensure that my idea is theologically sound and help me to develop it.

(2) The idea must be in accordance with the statements of faith of the church and its confession or deal with current social issues. This theological assessment is not some minor aspect of sermon preparation. The preacher must be aware of the fact that they are involved in the theological work of the church and its presence in society. Preachers represent the biblical and ecclesiastical tradition and must continually say things that may seem audacious when compared with the statements of faith of the church, the latest findings in the area of science and theology and the current concerns of the public. In the name of God, the preacher ventures into an open field without any protection. In this role, preachers can become the vanguard of theological work and forming of opinions. This applies to lay preachers as well as pastor, albeit in different ways.

3. GATHERING MATERIALS

Often, the idea will form the basis of only part of the final sermon. I have to place the idea into a wider context that makes it into a workable topic for a sermon. I may, for example, gather information on anti-authoritarian parenting, abortion, environmental issues - in general and in my hometown. Only if I have significant knowledge regarding these topics am I in a position to preach on them. I do not have to be an expert, but I ought to have an informed opinion of my own. I take a public stand, because, as a preacher, I fulfil a public role. **Third step**

I try to present my topic as vividly as possible. From then on, my sermon preparation follows the same order as for the route from the text to the sermon. I need to gather material. Material for the sermon topic may be obtained from two main areas:

(1) From my own experience. I tell the hearers about myself. The use of the first person pronoun in the sermon helps many hearers to identify with a topic, provided that they can identify with the personal experiences of the preacher. This aspect will be discussed in more depth in Chapters 7 and 8.

(2) I can also glean material from stories that I hear from others or read. I collect poems and pictures with meaning, and I look at sermons of others related to my topic.

I then write down the most important items I have found from both areas and collate them.

4. FORMULATING THE OBJECTIVES

Fourth step   At this point, I must determine what it is that I hope to achieve with my sermon, where I want to take my hearers, where I have to meet them in order to get to where I want them to go. I consider all this after having taken a break for inspiration.

5. COMPOSING THE SERMON

Fifth step   Now I have to evaluate my material in order to determine the best route to get to the goal of my sermon. Not everything that I have collected is suitable. The following points should be considered when selecting material:

(1) The examples and illustrations used in the sermon should carry weight and support the message of the sermon.

(2) The material used should be interesting and offer something fresh to the hearers: fresh information, new stories, original insights. Even amusing sections may be included to give the hearers something to laugh about.

(3) Examples and stories should be presented in a way that creates suspense. It should be a case of, "When the hearer looked at her watch after 10 minutes, she was surprised to notice that half an hour had already passed" rather than, "When the hearer looked at his watch after half an hour, he was surprised to notice that only 10 minutes had passed."

When putting together the sermon, it is important to have a clear organisational plan. The organisation must reflect the goal of the sermon and ensure that the individual building blocks of the sermon are connected in a meaningful way. More will be said on the structure and organisation in Chapter 4.

Sermon on the topic: hearing sermons (R. Lindner)

The following short sermon that I shared with a group of church social workers will mark the end of the route from the topic to the sermon. The idea came to me while meditating on the hearing of sermons. I wanted to find out how hearers react if they are addressed as experts in the area of hearing sermons. I wanted to express what they themselves can assess. My aim was to verify whether my ideas about hearers' expectations were correct.

I would like to preach to you this morning on the topic of hearing sermons. I therefore address you as experts. You have all heard many sermons in your lives. You have had experiences with sermons, both good and bad. You sense whether a sermon is good for you, whether it helps you. And you can tell if it means nothing to you. This is often the case. We preachers are aware of that. I often feel discouraged when a sermon has yet again failed. I then feel like quitting.

But can I quit, may I quit? You wait for a word for the week. You come expecting something important, including this morning.

I can address you as experts in hearing sermons. You can judge whether I describe it correctly. As I speak on this topic, some of you may ask yourselves: What scripture might such a sermon be based on? That is an important question. I have to answer it for you: I have been thinking about the words of the apostle Paul which he wrote in Romans: "Faith comes by hearing" (10:17).

1. As you have gathered together here this morning, I may assume that you want to hear. I assume that your motive is faith or, more precisely, the assurance of faith. That is what we need for the week, you and I. We need something to stand on, something to hold onto, clear direction, goals for what we do, something to help us make decisions. What can we expect from God in this regard, today and tomorrow?

I recently read about an old-fashioned doctor who had not changed his patient records to a card filing system. He wrote everything into a thick book. That was very impractical. At that time, there were already more efficient methods. What was special about the doctor's thick book was that these two words were written on the first page: "with God".

I would like to be so old-fashioned this morning as to write on the first page of my working week: with God. That helps me. How else shall I get through the week? So much is confusing. Many things just seem pointless to me. Where do I get the ability to decide correctly what is important and what isn't? Where do I get the calmness without which my work is nothing but hectic running up and down? That is why I want to have the words "with God" written on the first page of my week, this week and the weeks to come. These two words encourage me, they give me strength.

I need such an assurance of faith. It is good if I can get help. I assume that many of you feel the same way. That is why we listen to sermons: the assurance of faith comes by hearing. It enters through the ear and penetrates into the heart. It brings calm. Things become easier, the darkness of the night disappears, dawn breaks.

2. But we need more than just assurance. We need direction, direction for our thoughts, especially in Christian social work. Our day-to-day experience seems to preach so fervently against these two words: "with God". Is that not old-fashioned or, at least, irrelevant to our work? No! "With God" is the direction we need. That means: Yes, people should be at the centre of what we think and do. That seems reasonable. That is the right priority for all our work. So then, "with God" means: for the people with whom we spend this day, the people for whom we care. We need someone who keeps reminding us of this fact, because we have a natural tendency to forget, time and again. We need God's word, His question to us is: Do you love your neighbour? I have to respond to this by saying: I find it hard. That is why I need direction. Christian social work without God? No, that is impossible!

3. The right direction is closely connected with the right decision. This is the third thing that can come from hearing a sermon, as well as assurance and direction. In theory, we know all about loving our neighbour, being people-orientated. What we now need is to be challenged to do it. Something is set in motion, the bow is drawn, ready to launch the arrow in the direction of the target. The way I understand preaching is that you help me to find the right decisions like the arrow finds the target. And then I set off, resisting voices that try to dissuade me, over obstacles, through failures. A person who has heard God's challenge cannot easily be stopped. Such a person must follow and can follow His call, because he proceeds from God's peace and has been given the right direction by Him. Now he sends me on my way. I go: with God. You go: with God. We have a very present help. Amen.

Examining our example

We will now examine that which was said in the sermon according to the steps for the route from the topic to the sermon outlined above.

The idea

I was asking myself whether the hearers agree with my assumptions regarding their expectations. The idea came to me to present my thoughts to the hearers themselves. My topic was: Hearing sermons. Or more precisely: the hearer is my expert critic; he knows what helps him. I have arrived at this conclusion as a result of countless conversations about sermons. This is what I wanted to share with colleagues working in Christian care and social work. After the sermon, they confirmed to me that they consider these assumptions to be correct.

Theological questions

The idea was theologically substantiated. It can be related directly to Romans 10:17 and to many more biblical texts that describe hearing as a means to faith. Furthermore, the church is given the responsibility for proclaiming the gospel in accordance with the scriptures. The members of our congregations are becoming increasingly aware of this responsibility today and want to be addressed as mature Christians. This is their legitimate conviction, which I wanted to strengthen.

Gathering material

I was aware of the theoretical problems of my sermon. I had to find a way of bringing them across to the hearers. My choice of specific issues resulted from my own experience in Christian social work. The hearers have had similar experiences: they too doubt at times whether their work is really worthwhile. They are in danger of doing many things, but not the things for which they are really called. Impulses of the will often do not result in deeds.

Formulating the objectives

I wanted to inform the hearers of the three movements of seeking and areas of receiving involved in the hearing process and how they relate to their work: i.e. assurance, direction, and challenging to act (cf. Chapter 3). The result was the organisation of the sermon into three parts.

Composing the sermon

1. I made my selection from the material available with the intention to inform the hearers about things which they could immediately understand. I made reference to experiences which the hearers had acquired during many years of service. They became aware of the movements of seeking that keep recurring in their lives. They had an "aha-experience".

2. The hearers were motivated by the fact that they were being treated as experts and not as ignorant. The hearers' experiences agreed with my own.

Chapter 3: Preaching for hearers

Now that we have discussed the route from the text (or topic) to the sermon in the previous chapter we will focus on the hearers. After all, the sermon should effect something in the hearers, it should become the words of the one "who implanted the ear" (Ps. 94:9).

As in the rest of this section entitled "Practical manual"; our focus will be on general insights and practical tips. First, we want to bring out the fact that the preacher and the hearers share the responsibility for the preaching process; in the second section of this chapter we will then discuss three types of hearing; finally we will look at the consequences of our findings for our preaching.

In his paper "Pia desideria" (Godly desires, 1675), Philipp Jakob Spener, a theologian belonging to the German Pietist movement, wrote: "... the preacher must adapt his preaching to the hearers, as they cannot adapt themselves to him: his focus must always be mainly on the simple, so as to include most and not just a few learned ones."[1]

No matter whether we are preaching to the "simple" or the "learned", one fact always remains: we preach for our hearers! They should be able to receive and process the message of the sermon, and what they have heard should affect their lives. In order to ensure this, preachers need to have a better knowledge of the precepts and rules for "handling" their hearers when preaching.

I. Learning for the sermon

Preachers usually know a lot about their text, but often very little about their hearers. Hearers, on the other hand, are rarely **What do** able to say what exactly they "gain" from a sermon. This is what **hearers** the preacher needs to find out. By talking to the hearers, **gain from** preachers learn what effect the sermon has had. In doing so, they **a sermon?** may come to realise that the huge effort put into their sermons is not in vain. Preachers can learn something by ascertaining

---

1   Pia Desideria, Ed., by K. Aland, 1940, p. 79.

reactions from hearers and so learn how to get their message across better.

1. THE SHARED RESPONSIBILITY OF PREACHERS AND HEARERS

If preachers ask their hearers, why they want to hear sermons, how they receive them and process them and what they do with what they have heard they will usually get very vague answers. The hearers may, for example, confirm:

- that they have gained something from the sermon (but what?)
- that they like listening to the preacher (but why?)
- that they feel challenged (but what are the consequences?)

Some hearers who have nothing positive to say prefer to remain silent. Others want to voice their criticism to the preacher ("I didn't agree with what you said in your sermon today ..."), but find it hard to do so immediately after the sermon. The hearer senses that the preacher is very vulnerable. The preacher has just had to work hard and has, in both senses of the word, "given" something of him and must first "recover" from this before being able to react objectively to criticism. What must be considered as well is that if the preacher has not handled the hearers as successfully as he would have liked he will have an uneasy feeling. He is preoccupied with the question: How could I have better got the gospel across to my hearers? Like an athlete after a competition, the preacher needs to be given time. Hearers who want to offer constructive criticism sense this. In many churches, there are members of the congregation who are willing to bear the responsibility for the preaching with the preacher. Sometimes it may be the spouse of the preacher, or perhaps a close friend. There may be a group of sermon hearers who get together to discuss the preaching, or maybe there is an actual service preparation group who evaluate the service and correspond with the preacher. In Chapter 6, we will explain in more detail how this shared responsibility for the preaching process may be realised.

At this point, we will merely give some tips on how hearers can help their preacher. John Wesley (1703-1791), the founder of **How** the Methodist movement, is said to have read his (very lengthy!) **hearers** sermons to his maid before preaching them. Every preacher **can help** should really have the possibility of rehearsing a sermon **preachers** manuscript with someone or having someone read it without any problems. However, it would be even more useful if a group of church workers were already involved in preparing the service and the sermon. Praying together helps us to remember that, in the church service, it is God who serves us humans and not we who **Preparing** serve God. The group selects the topic or text for the sermon **the service** together. Preaching series are planned in advance and, when **together** planning the services, elements are included that will appeal to the congregation. The preacher can bring into the planning of the worship service what she wants to say in the sermon. Her partners may correct her or suggest changes. In some churches, it has been agreed that the sermon manuscript is always checked by the team members. The idea behind this is not to shut out the Holy Spirit, but to examine the sermon particularly with regard to hearer-orientation and to improve its quality in general. This approach is especially helpful when the sermon is specifically directed towards the unchurched.[2] Even though this shared sermon preparation requires time and energy, the benefits clearly outweigh the inconveniences: many issues can be resolved beforehand. As a **Where there** result, any discussions after the sermon has been preached are **is trust,** more objective. The mutual trust that exists within the group **there can** supporting the preacher makes it possible to voice criticism. This **be criticism** kind of help will allow the preacher to improve his/her preaching. The preacher's partners will also benefit: they will become better sermon hearers and will acquire more expertise in helping preachers fulfil their role.

---

2   It may also be helpful to have an abridged written version of the sermon that
    the hearers can take home. In addition, hearers could be given the
    opportunity to express their views in writing by way of a "feedback sheet".

2. EXPERIENCES REGARDING COLLABORATION BETWEEN PREACHERS AND HEARERS

Due to their different perspectives, preachers and hearers will have different questions regarding the composition and evaluation of the sermon.

Hearers want to know for example:

- Why did this sermon affect me? Why could I remember a lot of the sermon and why did it mean something to me?

- Why did the sermon upset me? Why did I get nothing out of it?

Preachers, on the other hand, want to know:

- Why was the congregation touched by my sermon? What is it about my sermon that made many of the hearers go home encouraged?

- Why did I not get any responses this time? Why does my sermon effect so little?

There are a number of answers that may be given to such questions. In the course of this chapter, we will introduce three types of speaking and hearing which can help to ensure that the sermon reaches its hearers. In chapter 7, the relationship between the preacher and the hearers and the effect of the sermon will be examined from the perspective of communication studies.

First, however, we would like you to reflect on your own personal experience with the help of the following exercise.

Write down what you think of when reading these questions:

✎ Exercise QUESTIONS FOR HEARERS

Consider how the preacher whom you hear regularly treats you as hearers:

- The sermon affects me / does not affect me, because ...

- I can / cannot follow the sermon, because ...

- The preacher addresses his/her hearers directly / is vague. I can tell this, because ...

- I would enjoy the sermon more if the preacher ...

- What did I do best the last time I preached / what didn't go so well?

- Where did I feel that the hearers were following what I was saying / where did I lose them?

- I found certain parts difficult when preparing the sermon. How did I manage these parts when delivering the sermon?

- Did I know what I wanted to achieve with the sermon, was I clear about my aim?

These questions may help hearers and preachers to become more aware of their experiences with preaching and with understanding the biblical message together. Preachers and hearers can gain something from this, both for themselves and for their part of the preaching process. If these experiences can be shared within a group consisting of preachers and hearers, then both parties, preachers and hearers, can together become experts in the field of preaching communication. They can both learn something, which will enable them to fulfil their shared responsibility for the preaching process more effectively, and consequently to discuss any issues as partners. In order for this process to be successful, the expectations of the sermon must be clear.

II. Expectations of the sermon

1 THE SERMON - BETTER THAN ITS REPUTATION

For some time, theologians everywhere have been talking about a "crisis of preaching". Some even believe that it would be **The crisis** best to stop the "ailing" business of preaching altogether. The **of** doubts are deep. Theological arguments intended to dispel these **preaching** doubts are not normally perceived as being of much help. There must be a different way of helping the preachers who have to stand in the pulpit again on Sunday morning. If it is clear that they can learn something new that will benefit their preaching and therefore experience a feeling of "success" they will begin to enjoy their work again. This is where the shared responsibility for the sermon

71

through prayer and discussion described above has its place. The preacher is no longer paralysed as much by doubts concerning the point of preaching. They are left only with the inevitable doubts concerning their work. They are prevented from becoming overly self-confident and remain conscious of the fact that they do not have God's voice at their disposal.

There is another reason why it makes sense to preach, besides the fact that the preacher can learn something from it to improve their sermons: the fact that people want to hear sermons. The following information may surprise some: on an average Sunday morning an estimated one million Germans hear a sermon in a service of the Lutheran church (K.-W. Dahm); according to a recent survey, a further three quarters of a million people hear sermons in independent Protestant churches. These figures neither include non-Protestant church traditions nor the hearers and viewers of preaching programmes broadcast on radio and television and the readers of "thoughts for the day" published in magazines and newspapers, which may also be regarded as "sermons".

There is a demand for good sermons Although it is difficult to obtain accurate data in this regard and there may be various reasons why people attend church services, one thing is indisputable: preaching is evidently not as bad as its reputation. There is a demand, a need for good sermons, which are biblically sound and relevant to the lives of the hearers. Many Christians want "to get something out of the sermon", to be able to follow it consciously, to receive it and to process it. Due to this increased awareness on the part of the hearers, it is necessary for the preacher to speak in a way that will encourage people to listen.

We will now take a closer look at the interest people have in preaching. Why do so many people want to hear a sermon? We may suggest the following reasons:

• The hearers feel that they have a need.

• Based on past experience, the hearers expect the sermon to be able to satisfy that need, at least to some extent.

Generally speaking, we may assume that only people who have a specific need and know that they can find what they need in the church service and in the sermon will be prepared to listen. A person who wants to hear will not normally be put off for very long from listening to sermons even if they had repeatedly had negative experiences in the past. Many have asserted more than once in their anger that they would never again set foot in a church and yet returned after a while. A hearer will not easily be discouraged from an expectation that the sermon will satisfy their need; for the yearning and searching for security and orientation in life which many people experience today is directed towards God and God can speak and work in church either through the sermon or through other parts of the service.

2. TYPES OF SPEAKING AND HEARING

A condition of need usually leads to seeking actions. This is a **Seeking** general pattern of human behaviour. A person who is cold wants **actions of** to warm himself. A hungry person wants to eat. In the same way, **the hearers** people who want to hear sermons are in search of something specific. The way this search is conducted may differ from one person to another. Nonetheless, we can identify certain types of searches. These different types can, however, only be described schematically. The same applies to types of discourse that correspond to the various seeking actions of the hearers. The types of hearing and speaking may be described on the basis of the experiences that speakers have had in dealing with their hearers over the years. It must be noted, however, that these types usually occur in hybrid forms. An individual will embody a measure of each of the three speaking and hearing types. Consequently, every hearer and every preacher will have their own profile, their own way of listening and speaking. Certain aspects may, however, sometimes be more pronounced than others, depending on the situations in which individuals find themselves.

On the following pages, hearers will find described what they seek in a sermon and what irritates them about a particular type of discourse. With the help of this description, the hearer can recognise the need that triggers a particular seeking action. Preachers, too, will be able to identify which ways of speaking cause their preaching to be successful and which ones do not. Each preacher has a particular rhetorical expression. As they become acquainted with other types of discourse, they can try to learn them. This will help preachers to reach more people and open up more and wider "reception areas" for them. The hearers and preachers can add to their range. They can learn to hear and speak better.

In the following, three types of speaking and hearing will be described. These three types each appeal to different "reception areas" of the human consciousness and consequently have different effects.

The types of discourse described below were already known in Ancient Greece; the Greek philosopher Aristotle described them in his treatise entitled "Rhetoric". While Plato had previously dismissed the art of speaking as an "art of flattery", Aristotle believed that rhetoric was essential to "good living" in any human society.

Seeking actions of hearers	Reference to time	Relevant types of discourse	Reception areas in hearers
Meaning of life	Present	epideictic	emotions
Orientation	Past	judicial	mind
Decision	Future	deliberative	will

Demonstrative discourse

- Epideictic (or demonstrative) discourse was used to acknowledge the achievements of a statesman or scientist

Informative discourse

- Judicial (or informative) discourse was used in court in order to help the judge through evidence and argumentation to pass a just sentence

Challenging discourse

- Deliberative (or challenging) discourse was used in political gatherings. The hearers were challenged to choose a political party and to act in accordance with his choice.

These types of discourse are not simply the construct of a philosopher, but an aggregation of experiences which speakers have had in dealing with their hearers in particular situations. The speaker uses them to achieve a particular effect. In the following, we will show how these classical types of discourse can be applied to preaching, where the conditions are quite different.

a) The reception area of the emotions

In the present situation, a lack of security is probably the most important motive for expecting something from a sermon (cf. Chapter 1). The hearer does not know what standards to live by. They have no confidence in their world. They question the world in which they live. A particular incident has caused them to feel insecure. Therefore they are looking for firm ground on which to stand. Or the hearer has experienced minor or major disappointments: failure at work, problems with their children, fear of things that lie ahead. They are no longer sure about the meaning of life. They cannot cope alone anymore.

The search for a meaning in life

People who are in search of meaning in their lives come to church. They are looking for a place where they can find tranquillity and shelter. They want to regain any confidence they may have lost. Does the faith that they have had thus far still work? Occasional doubts and the constant anti-sermon of their everyday lives have caused them to question its relevance. The regular hearer encounters many opinions that contradict their faith.

Seeking assurance

EXAMPLE: *It's Sunday morning and a woman has just been told by her husband: "So you're going to church again. What is it doing for you?" On her way to church, this woman will wonder whether her husband may be right and whether she would be better off staying doing what many people do: sleeping in on a Sunday morning or taking a trip to the countryside. In this emotional condition the woman comes to church looking for help. She expects the preacher to restore her to a place of security in the faith, something that she cannot find with her husband or with other people. By taking part in the church service, she hopes to be restored as a child of God. Together with other people who come expecting their faith to be strengthened, she wants to be able to breathe freely, relieved from the storm of contradictions against her faith. She wants to "fill up" in order to be prepared for the uncertain days that lie ahead.*

However, the hearer who comes to church from the dull routine of the week seeks more than tranquillity and security. They seek not only assurance and edification, but also a powerful uplifting and the joy of celebration. They want the dark thoughts to be dispelled by strong light. The hearer wants to leave the past behind and not have to worry about what lies ahead. During this hour, they want to celebrate, to be able to satisfy their yearning, to be close to the manifest move of God.

Trying to determine the effects of a feast-day sermon on the hearers would be taking the discussion too far. The experience of such an occasion is valuable in itself. We cannot judge it by its usefulness, as we would not judge an uplifting holiday or a beautiful concert by its "success". The aesthetic experience alone makes it valuable. What must also be considered is the fact that re-orientation is usually only possible if the individual concerned has (re) discovered him/herself. It is then that they can be challenged to take the first steps in a different direction. An individual must first stand on their feet, before being able to look around and move forward.

☍ **Exercise** QUESTION FOR HEARERS: You probably remember specific situations in your life where a sermon helped you. Try to describe the need that you experienced at the time and what you remember of the sermon, what type of sermon it was, its content, and the preacher (their voice, personal appearance, style of preaching).

QUESTION FOR PREACHERS: Describe how you react when someone comes up to you after the service to express appreciation, saying: "That was a lovely sermon today!" or "The service was so touching today!" What do you think of the feelings expressed by the grateful hearer and your reaction to it?

76

A person who is searching for meaning in life and has the experience of finding firm ground to stand on and being edified and uplifted will be touched first and foremost in their emotions. A very unemotional church service and a teaching sermon on problems that do not affect the hearer directly will not appeal to them. The rational world in which the hearer lives already makes strong demands on their mind. In the service, their will is not waiting to be set new tasks. A person who has had to work hard all week wants to be able to sit back on a Sunday morning and take in something positive.

Many hearers can be most easily reached through the reception area of the emotions. They are not so much "mind people" or "will people" but rather "emotions people". They experience the world around them not primarily through the actions of the mind or will, in other words, not in a logical order. Neither are they constantly trying to establish such a logical order. Instead, they experience the world in moments, in pictures, in moods. They register the things they encounter primarily in the sphere of their emotions: in the form of worry, fear, aggression, sorrow, compassion, dedication, joy. They want to be edified and uplifted so they can see the meaning behind the things that affect their lives, not through their minds but through their hearts. What they are looking for is not instruction or admonition, but "spirituality", a spiritual experience that affects the whole person. **"Emotions people"**

Demonstrative discourse

There are more people who belong to this type of hearer than most Protestant preachers generally assume. Preachers often act in an unemotional, didactic manner, suppressing the sphere of the emotions. They feel that the sermon should not be beautiful and touching but serious and full of substance. Without being aware of it, many preachers believe that it is enough to expound the content of a passage of scripture properly; the hearers will understand themselves what it is all about. This idea, however, is wrong. At least at the beginning of a sermon, the preacher should look out for the seeking actions of the hearers in the emotional **"Picking up" the hearers**

77

sphere in order to be able to pick them up at that point and to lead them on from there.

The preacher and the hearer searching for meaning in life can meet and communicate. The demonstrative discourse is particularly suited for this purpose. A preacher who is aware of the hearer situation will immediately come up with a series of bible passages that will comfort, encourage and impart joy. Here are some examples:

- "Even though I walk through the valley of the shadow of death, I will fear no evil, for you are with me." (Ps. 23:4)

- "Praise the LORD, oh my soul, all my innermost being, praise his holy name." (Ps. 103:1)

- "In this world you will have trouble. But take heart! I have overcome the world." (John 16:33)

- "Blessed are the poor in spirit, for theirs is the kingdom of heaven." (Matt. 5:3)

- "If God is for us, who can be against us?" (Rom. 8:31)

- "Then I saw a new heaven and a new earth, ..." (Rev. 21:1)

In a bible concordance we can find under the headings *fear, worry, comfort, help, love, rejoice, praise* an abundance of scriptures that will speak directly to people who are searching for meaning in life and give preachers necessary inspiration for demonstrative discourse.

The bible passage and the type of discourse should agree
The bible passage and the type of discourse should agree. The preacher must therefore consider not only the expectations of the hearers and their need, but also the form of the text to be able to convey the content in an appropriate manner. If, for example, I were to use Psalm 8 as the basis for discussion of the relationship between theology and science, I would be violating this hymn to creation. The account of creation in Genesis 1 with its didactic form would be more suitable for such a topic.

The following example illustrates how the health resort preacher Wilhelm Knuth tried to adapt the form of his sermon to

78

the bible passage of Luke 12:22-31. He took his hearers - vacationers on a North Sea island - out of the church so as to let nature become a parable to them of the Father's care and provision for the people of little faith too. In the sermon, the preacher relates the picture of the lilies and the grass of the field to the marram grass and praises God who cares for the grass, the dunes and even more so for the people:

"Consider the marram grass! As small and insignificant as it may seem, it fulfils its purpose. It prevents the dangerous drifting dunes from developing and thus protects the woodland and fields from the sand. How can it live in the blazing heat of the sun on the dry drifting sand? It has roots that are more than ten times as long as those of the green grass do. They get their nourishment from the deep. Only if the wind manages to seize the dune from the bottom, at the roots of the marram, is it able to carry it away. The marram grass is able to solve its problems - so should there not be a source in the deep for us humans too from which we can draw what we need to live?

Our holiday will have been a success if we can be shown the way out of the difficulties of life. This way has already been prepared for us by God. Also, he has long provided a firm foundation and a source for us in his word. He himself is the source of our being. God is surely more interested in his children than in the rest of nature. If he can arrange the environment for the smallest of creatures in such a wonderful way, he will surely have a plan prepared for our lives that is good for us. When Jesus tells us to consider nature, he does not mean simply to enjoy the beauty of nature or to examine it biologically; he wants us to learn its language of symbols. This language is not only spoken by nature and can be heard not just whilst on holiday. We will progress step by step if we apply what we have learnt here in our everyday lives and in the concrete jungle of our cities. We will be healed if we learn to recognise the loving care and provision of the father in our own lives. Then our criticism of his ruling over our lives will be transformed into the trust of a child who is secure in the father's arms."[3]

---

3   W. Knuth, Zwischen Sorge und Freude, Gladbeck 1973, p. 12.

This sermon extract is interesting, because it shows the overlap of two types of discourse. The picture of the marram grass, which is meant as a stimulus for meditation, becomes the master who teaches against worrying (informative, explanatory). Preachers have many means for meditative preaching at their disposal. They can also use their own situation without God's saving grace as a parable. A wife and mother put it like this:

I am often overcome by fear. I feel like I am standing on a thin layer of ice that is already beginning to crack. I am threatened on every side.

My husband - might he get killed in an accident? My children - what will become of them in this sinister world? My friend - she has cancer and has only a few more months to live. Tomorrow, it might be me.

Sometimes I stand in front of the mirror anxiously searching for any wrinkles that might be showing in my face. What will I look like when I am 60 or 70? Bitter, careworn or wise and cheerful?

Some day this face will no longer smile or weep, some day it will be rigid, turn into dust. My face is only lent to me, just like my life. A gift that I can either waste or make use of.

This is not an "aesthetic speech" as it was practised in ancient Greek rhetoric. It does not celebrate woman in her glory, but describes her in her fear. Humanity is not exalted by it. It is about being raised from the deep by God's saving hand, for which the resurrection of Jesus Christ from the dead is our assurance for all time. As this brings comfort to the hearers, we do not have to pretend anything to them when it comes to their situation without God's saving grace.

The hearers and the preacher stand together before God
The hearer finds it harder to identify with the preacher if, like this woman, she speaks openly in the first person *"I"* and in the present tense *(I am often overcome ... I feel ..., sometimes I stand in front of the mirror ...")*. This brings the preacher and the hearer very close to one another. That moment, both are standing before God. The preacher's words can lead on to a prayer without any difficulty. This is what we read in the psalms. Those who pray and profess the words of the psalm describe their hopeless situation and

80

their deliverance from affliction (e.g. Psalm 22). A person is plucked out of their state, being forsaken by God and consequently praise God for answering their prayer (vv.20-25).

The following extract from a Christmas sermon by Bernhard Fitzke is yet another example of how easily the hearer can identify with the "I" of the preacher. After having learnt the different types of discourse, he composed a pure form of demonstrative sermon:

"Do not be afraid!" an angel said.

Am I afraid?

"I bring you good news of joy. Today a saviour has been born to you."

All I see is a pitiful stable.

"He is Christ the Lord."

Have I not already got enough lords? How I would love to believe the angel! How I would love to go to Bethlehem! ...

It is only with reluctance that I take the first steps towards Bethlehem. After a while, my steps get faster, because I didn't like the place from which I am coming. But do I know where I will end up? I stand in front of the stable; above it I see the star, familiar and yet strange. I enter. Mother and child, the manger, it is not for the first time that I see all this, everything is just the way it has been affectionately painted and described by thousands over the centuries. Everything looks familiar to me, but I now see it with different eyes. The dark stable is bright. My eyes have been opened, lit by the gleam of light which proceeds from the manger, and it is only now that I perceive in horror the darkness from which I have come. What appeared as light to me was really the cloak of darkness, the veil of obscurity, my ruin. But the veil is torn, from top to bottom: here I find light!"

The preacher tries to liberate hearers from their darkness and to lead them into the light of the gospel. The congregation will then be able to sing a hymn with great joy. The preacher's words and the worship become one. The preacher is not a lonesome soloist but is included in the worship of the congregation. They are both preacher and member of the congregation. Like the other members of the congregation, they contribute to the success of the worship service. Both the worship and the sermon involve the congregation.

Here is another exercise:

☛ **Exercise** QUESTION FOR HEARERS: What were you touched by as you read these sermon extracts? What appealed to you / what bothered you?

QUESTION FOR PREACHERS: Can you preach in a way that encourages people and gives them joy?

Check some of your preaching manuscripts. Which type of preaching do you find easier: referring to examples of others or speaking about your own experiences? Do you think that you could adopt ways of speaking that do not come to you naturally?

b) The reception area of the mind

The search for meaning in life and the corresponding demonstrative discourse is all about people being able to get up on their feet again. The aim must be to edify and lift them, to strengthen them and liberate them from the pressures that weigh them down. This psychological relief and strengthening is an important aspect. However, a person who has been helped out of the pit of spiritual and emotional low also needs to be informed about the reason why God helps them in this time of need and where they can find firm ground from which to proceed further. A preacher will therefore seek to appeal to the mind as well as the emotions. It is not enough for the people attending the service to be drawn into a festive tranquillity. They should learn to find their way in the world in which they live. The hearers should not merely stand on their feet; they should also look around and then move forward.

The search for direction

If people lack meaning in life they are usually not able to take in any new information. They cannot see anything, because they are surrounded by darkness. They therefore search for light. If they find this light they often think they now have everything.

They feel satisfied that they have found what they were looking for. This applies to many hearers. It is not easy to lead them on any further. As leading people on from where they are is a central objective of Christian preaching, the preacher must work diligently to ensure that hearers who are governed primarily by their emotions continue their search. They need more than just the strengthening of their faith. They should grow in faith, learn something new, and extend the horizons of their lives.

Beside these "emotions people", there is another kind of hearer, whose main aim is to learn something from the sermon. These are "mind people". They want logical conclusive arguments in favour of the Christian faith. They too need something. They are used to understanding the world through the mind. When it comes to matters of faith, however, this is often not possible for them. That is why they come to hear a sermon, to find answers. An individual may, for example, no longer understand particular issues in their life. They cannot make sense of them and want to gain an overview, to be able to see through things, to assess and sort the things that they do not understand. Maybe the information they have had thus far regarding faith and Christian living has come to naught. What they now want to know is: How can my faith be re-established, how can I grow in faith? **"Mind people"**

The hearer wants information that they can comprehend with the mind and that they can expound to others clearly through logical reasoning. They want to know how their present life relates to the past, to tradition. For this purpose, they need information, interpretations that can withstand the criticism of reason. The adolescent daughter has argued against the father or the mother: "The pastor and his stories of miracles - those are all fairy tales that sensible people can't be expected to believe!" The parents therefore search for information regarding the meaning of Jesus' miracles today. In this condition of uncertainty, the preacher may help the hearer by telling them how they understand the accounts of miracles, where they feature in their conception of the world. Even if the hearer then comes to the conclusion that they cannot see it the way the preacher sees it, because many things remain unclear in their mind, they will respect the preacher's attempt at resolving the issue. The hearer expects a solution with a personal touch, a confession based on information about faith and life.

Thus, a search for direction cannot be satisfied merely by factual information. Logical statements and clearly defined terms alone will not do. The hearer expects something different from the sermon than they would expect from a theological lecture. Many preachers find this difficult. They may present theological information in a theologically sound way, the sermon may turn out "dead right" (Rudolf Bohren). However, they are keenly aware that very little of it is received. Evidently the big words of the bible are too heavy for the hearers. They are more like stones than like bread. The preaching of the gospel, in contrast, is like a sumptuous meal for which the hearers gladly accept an invitation. If the guests stay away the hosts, the preachers, often resign. Many ask themselves: is there no hunger among the people for the truth of the gospel? (cf. Am. 8:11)

Informative discourse

The same principle that applies to people who are
Conveying approachable primarily in reception area of their emotions is also
faith valid for people who comprehend the world through their minds.
information They need to be spoken to in a way that will convey information regarding the Christian faith from the preacher to the hearer. This is not easy. That is why some hearers who need arguments in favour of the Christian faith will prefer a group discussion. Nonetheless, this can be achieved as well through a sermon.

The following two examples are instances of informative discourse. As with all examples, the purpose is to encourage a critical analysis.

In a sermon on the virgin birth of Jesus Christ, Bishop Hans Lilje illustrates how a difficult dogmatic statement may be conveyed to the reader.[4] At the beginning of his sermon, Bishop

---

4   Printed in: H.-R. Müller-Schwefe, Zur Zeit oder Unzeit, Stuttgart 1958, pp. 47-55.

Lilje responds to the critical questions of his hearers regarding this "incredible story" and refutes existing misunderstandings, and then goes on to explain why in our confession of the Virgin Mary we have the "guarantee of our salvation". Bishop Lilje presents his information to the hearers so as to allow them to judge for themselves:

"Firstly, our Lord Jesus Christ entered into our earthy world. He was born. He became a man. He did the inconceivable in taking our entire human fate upon himself. As much as they may talk about the incarnation of their gods, none of the world religions has dared to say to us what Christians confess of their Lord: that he became as one of us.

This means: We have not been left alone in the turmoil of violence, guilt, fear in life and fear of death. God is there. Jesus has come to us.

Secondly, however, this portion of the gospel testifies to us of something that is equally important: Jesus did not merely become our "mate", but our Saviour. And this was possible, because he was not of our nature or of our world.

Everything depends on this. That is why the preaching of a Christ who is of our nature was such an elementary misunderstanding of the Christian message. It is precisely on this fact that everything, absolutely everything depends: the fact that he is not of our nature - God from God, light from light, as the old Nicean creed declares."

Many preachers find it difficult to argue in such a dogmatic manner. They believe that the hearers cannot be reached with "eternal truths from above". For this reason, a way of speaking was developed at the preaching seminary Loccum which is meant to encourage the hearers to search. They should be able to follow the thoughts of the preacher, in order to come to a decision like a judge in a court case. Horst Hirschler produced a draft on the topic of "celebrating Christmas", which effectively illustrates this approach and will therefore serve as our second example.[5]

Encouraging hearers to judge for themselves

---

5   Werkstatt predigt I/1973, p. 3f.

"The meeting of the youth group had begun as usual. First, only three were present; within the next hour, the remaining eight girls and boys had arrived. We spoke about what the members of a particular Berlin church were doing during the Advent season. Someone had received a leaflet from them in the post. On it was printed in bold letters: "Operation Critical Christmas. Return from the consumerist orgy to the Christian celebration of Jesus' birth. Do not buy all that you want to buy!" Part of the money intended for Christmas shopping was requested for a teacher-training centre in Africa. We discussed the leaflet.

Suddenly, we found ourselves talking about Christmas in our own families. It's just boring, they said. One boy commented: It's fine when we open the presents, but later everybody sits in a corner with some book and that's it. A girl told us: In our family it's awful as well. My two brothers come with their wives and then we talk about their business the whole time. And our granny comes. Sometimes she can actually be quite okay. My brothers never want to go to church, never mind sing carols. But my granny always says: Children, you don't know how much longer I'll live. This may be my last Christmas. So sing a few of those nice carols for me, will you? And then we all have to sit down. She hands out the hymnbooks and we sing one carol after another. I don't even mind that so much. But later, after the dinner, there's nothing at all. - In fact, no one really had anything good to say about Christmas, even when I specifically asked them.

And then one of them suggested: Why don't we celebrate Christmas here as a youth group...? We could meet here around half past three, four o'clock in the afternoon. By that time it will all be over at home. And then we'll do our own "Operation Christian Christmas". At home, they wouldn't be interested anyway. Last time I wanted to read a modern Christmas story to them, but they didn't want to know. We could decorate the room nicely. - I'll get us a Christmas tree, someone butted in. We'll bring some music. And read something decent. We can play games ...

I didn't feel too good about it. The activity sounded good. But did it have to be on Christmas day? Weren't they supposed to spend Christmas with their families? Or was that idea too old-fashioned. After all, in many families, it really is a problem. What do we do at Christmas? Who decides on the programme? Is there really a programme? Adults are often afraid of the criticism of their children. But they, in turn, feel that they don't get a fair deal. The discussion at the youth meeting had consequences: I received several phone calls from angry parents. There was one good discussion involving two families about what it was that each side expected of Christmas.

What is a Christian Christmas really? Does it involve singing Christmas carols? Should there be a scripture reading? What would be appropriate to celebrate Jesus' birth? Allowing each generation to celebrate with their peers, separately? It might be necessary for a change; I discovered that when I recently spoke to parents of nearly grown-up children who told me: Ours aren't coming this year. We thought we'd each celebrate Christmas the way we want to. We're glad that we don't have to dance to the tune of our critical kids for a change.

But maybe Christmas is a good opportunity, after all, to spend time with each other. If the old and the young try to listen to one another, just to accept one another, that would fit Jesus' style very well.

The planned Christmas party was called off in the end. Mainly, because the plan had triggered off a discussion in the families about what they could do over Christmas. One family even decided to invite an African student to spend a few days with them. That was a good idea."

This sermon has a particular structure, which will be further explained in the next chapter. The point here was to show how the sermon can help hearers to form an opinion, how they can find their own way to a true "Christian Christmas".

Here is another exercise:

QUESTION FOR HEARERS: Describe what you feel when you read the above sermon extracts. What appeals to you / what doesn't?   ✑ **Exercise**

QUESTION FOR PREACHERS: Which way of speaking comes to you more easily: dogmatic informative way or the search for direction together with the hearers?

c) The reception area of the will

Search for help regarding decisions A person who can stand on their feet and look around is able to go forward of their own accord, to take steps of faith. They feel strengthened and informed about the foundations of the Christian faith. They may now be able to explain these to others in a logical way. This, however, does not necessarily mean that the hearers and the preacher act in accordance with what they know and live the Christian faith, for example by showing love to others, by caring for them in a practical way. Through the sermon, they themselves have experienced the security of love in their innermost being. However, their will has not yet received the impulse to pass on the love they have received in a specific way to specific individuals, to take up the future that has been promised in order to use it creatively. This can be effected through a challenging way of speaking within the reception area of the will.

The search for a decision

Especially young hearers often become impatient if the preacher spends a lot of time on meditative reflection and information about the faith. But there are also other people who understand the world primarily through their will and want an answer: What does that mean in practice, how can Christian faith be lived? Preachers often fail to give answers to these questions, or if they do, then usually at the end of the sermon in a few general **"Will people"** statements. The hearers feel that they are "beating around the bush", which is unsatisfactory to them. "Will people" are therefore disappointed and sometimes prefer to get involved in action groups in order to do project work.

There may be quite a number of people in the congregation who are looking for help with practical decisions regarding their present and future. Preachers will recognise this if they get told once in a while: "I followed your advice and did such and such." The preacher may have made some general remarks and is surprised to find out how these words were taken in a very different way than they were meant. In the sermon, the hearer who needed to make a decision received an impetus in a particular direction. Thus, the sermon has released the hearer to act, because they have related what was said to their situation and developed it further.

Such reactions reveal that something is lacking: Many hearers miss a stimulus for putting their faith into practice. Many know what good could be done, but fail to do it, because they do not have the courage or they are unsure, whether they are able to carry it out. This applies especially to big decisions. Many hearers know: If I want to take the sermon seriously I will have to change my life completely; but I haven't got the courage to do what others have done.

It is like the two boys who climbed onto a wall and got into danger up there. A man called to them: "Jump into my arms!" The one boy jumped and was caught safely. The man who had called was his father. The power of trust that drew him into the saving arms. The other boy had to be taken down from the wall by firefighters.

This issue features in many evangelistic sermons. The **Decision** evangelist Charles H. Spurgeon (1834-1892) once used it to **for** challenge his hearers to make a decision for Christ. In the sermon, **Christ** he urged his hearers:

"Oh, I beseech you by him whose heart is love, the crucified Redeemer, who now speaks through me this morning, and in me weeps over you, I beseech you look to him and be saved, for he came into the world to seek and to save that which was lost, and him that cometh to him he will in nowise cast out, for "he is able also to save them to the uttermost that come unto God by him."

Today, O Spirit bring sinners to thyself. I exhort you, sinners, lay hold on Christ. Touch the hem of his garment now. Behold, he hangs before you on the cross. As Moses lifted up the serpent in the wilderness ... even so is Jesus lifted up. Look, I beseech you, look and live. Believe on the Lord Jesus Christ and you shall be saved. As though God did beseech you by me, I pray you in Christ's stead be ye reconciled to God."

Challenging discourse

There is often no call to faith

Sermons often fail to call for a decision, at least the ones preached in regular Sunday services. Time and again, we are told that calling people to the faith is "not in keeping with the times". Many people are offended more by evangelistic activities with the aim of spreading the gospel than by the de facto spread of unbelief within large sections of our society. If we ask critics of evangelistic outreach and faith generating preaching for alternatives, they do not usually have anything to offer. In recent times, there has been a rediscovery of the great commission of the church in the independent Protestant churches. All Christian denominations are striving for a new evangelistic consciousness

Evangelism should become the rule

and seeking new ways of reaching those who have become alienated from the Christian faith. Evangelism should no longer be an exception, but the rule in the work of the church. In these evangelistic activities, the focus is (once more) increasingly on the ecumenical dimension.

In the context of preaching, challenging discourse is the most difficult of all. It requires good rhetorical skills and great sensitivity when it comes to appeals in the sermon (see Chapter 7). Many preachers shy away from challenging discourse, because they do not want to "put pressure" on their hearers. Another reason for the reluctance of preachers to challenge might be the fact that many hearers evade the challenge of faith in Christ. The help offered by the preacher is rejected. They urge them, but they don't want to hear. The individual who is addressed directly does not dare to jump even though assured through comforting words that they will land safely in the father's arms. This is what Jesus experienced with the rich young ruler whom he invited to follow him (Mark 10:17-27). The man decided against it. Jesus had left

Do not manipulate

the decision up to him. For challenging discourse, this means: the preacher must not force the hearer to make a particular decision nor seek to manipulate them in any way.

90

The Swiss writer Kurt Marti did not do this in his interpretation of the rich young ruler. The sermon reaches its climax with the statement by the evangelist Mark: Jesus looked at him and loved him (v.21).

"At this point I could really conclude the sermon with an Amen. Is there anything more and better than Jesus loving a person? That is everything, the last and the greatest thing that can happen to us. If Jesus looks at us today and loves us, then this Sunday is a feast unlike any other; we are 'cleaned and shined' right through to our hearts; we can then go happily on our way, nothing can befall us any more, we are saved for all eternity. And I really do believe that there are many present today in which Jesus takes pleasure, because they have not aborted the hunger in their innermost being for the living God. I also believe that there are many who are not here and do not go to church at all, but nonetheless are running around, seeking to satisfy this hunger. They too are loved by Jesus, because of their restlessness. It is for us to tell them.

But I still can't say Amen, because our story goes on, because the love of Jesus also goes further, presses further into our lives. That is why he says to that man whom he loves: 'One thing you lack. Go, sell everything you have and give to the poor, and you will have treasure in heaven... Then come, follow me.'

Jesus' love goes further than we think. Here, however, it seems to go too far. That is why this story doesn't have a happy ending. That is why it ends on an uncomfortable note. Everyone of us responds in the same way: that is going too far for me: 'Come, follow me.' I could accept that, because nowadays we can imagine following Jesus as a matter of the mind. But 'sell everything you have ...' no, that is going too far, that cannot be expected ...'[6]

The difficulty of challenging discourse lies in the fact that it is directed towards the future. The hearer is to make a decision for the future. They doubt whether this decision is right. Is it worth the cost, is it possible to reach the goal set by the preacher? The preacher, too, is often not sure. The hearer is making promises for the future. With informative discourse, it is easier. It talks about

Directed towards the future

---

6   K. Marti, Das Markus-Evangelium, Basel 1967, pp. 214-218.

the past, about history or previously acquired knowledge. Demonstrative discourse focuses on the present. It seeks closeness with God and the people who are present and to whom the preacher wants to be close.

Challenging discourse must be specific

Experience shows that challenging discourse is received best if it succeeds in finding, together with the hearer, the point from which they can dare to jump. If we call people to make a decision we must also be able to tell them how they should live their lives following Jesus after they have made a decision. Challenging discourse must be specific. For this reason, some evangelistic preachers will lead those who are ready to take the step of faith in a "prayer of salvation" in which they "give their lives to Jesus". Others call the hearers to "come to the front" so as to make a public confession of their new-found faith. Some evangelists invite those who respond to a personal conversation. The idea is to encourage the hearers to take initial steps of faith in an intimate, secure environment. This can take the form of a confession, a prayer, or a blessing. An approach that has proved increasingly successful in recent years is to invite people to take part in a "foundation course" in the Christian faith, at the end of which they are given an opportunity to commit their lives to God in a relaxed atmosphere.[7]

A destination requires a path

Any evangelistic endeavours must include specific advice as to what the people who are reached with the gospel and generally willing to (re-) commit their lives to God can do from then on. Depending on the situation, a suitable format will be found: what is important is that it happens at all. If preachers merely call for a decision regarding a very important matter without showing ways how precisely this can be done, it will leave their hearers in a grave state of uncertainty. The appeal gets nowhere and may, in the long term, lead to the hearers becoming "immune" to the claim of gospel.

The same applies to political sermons. They must stimulate the hearers to action that can be realised in practice: collection of

---

7   Cf. "Disciple Bible Studies", "Chrysalis", "Alpha", "Emmaus" and others.

signatures, public rallies and symbolic acts. Otherwise those involved will be discouraged or resort to a dangerous actionism. The problems of the political sermon are similar to those of the evangelistic sermon, as they are both instances of challenging discourse.

During his professorship of theology in Berlin, Helmut Gollwitzer suggested some concrete activities in his political sermons. The references to the political events of his time are clearly recognisable. Time and again, Gollwitzer addresses the individual hearer. If the individual will change, this can have far-reaching personal and political consequences. The hearer's consciousness is changed.

"Jesus says: Ask yourself, what you really lack, what you desperately need, what you are crying out for, what you painfully miss. You may be a very lonely person, you may long, as for your daily bread, for another person who will take care of you, who will listen to you and understand you. Be to the people around you the person that you need - Jesus says - and your loneliness will come to an end. You may be longing for a different spouse, one who is not so selfish, one who is joyful and caring. Be to your spouse the spouse that you long for - Jesus says - and many things will be different in your marriage. You are living in the treadmill of a job that you hate, that leaves you feeling empty. Look around, see how the others in your office and company feel just like you do, and be a person who brings a fresh atmosphere or even a fresh content to that treadmill that you cannot change! Being to others what you need from the others - that is the message of Jesus that, like a key, opens up the door to the lives of other people.

It is strange: By looking at yourself, you see others with their needs, you become aware of them. And then you will see: they are suffering even more from a lack of the things that you lack: you need money, you can't afford the things you need, but around you there are many who have even less. You need freedom, justice, a free democratic state under the rule of law and you are grateful if you can live in such a state. In Persian and Turkish prisons, they are tortured and sentenced to death. You need the freedom to openly express your opinion, your political and religious views. In Czechoslovakia, in Greece they are gagged.

You are a South African or a Rhodesian White with a house and a garden; the world is open to you. And beside you are the others, with a different colour, fourth class citizens, expelled from their land, they need the same things that you have. "So in everything, do to others what you would have them do to you, for this sums up the Law and the Prophets (Matt. 7:12)."[8]

If we make ourselves aware of the difficulties of the challenging sermon we can preach it in a responsible way. We need courage or, as the fathers and mothers in the faith say, authority. Because we are gripped by God, we can stand up for him and challenge our hearers to act. We can speak with the authority of the imploring Christ (2 Cor. 5:20). The preacher needs the presence of the Spirit and presence of mind, and also a great sensitivity to speak the right word at the right time. This word is aimed at that which yet lies ahead: following Jesus, changes in the present world, proceeding into an unpredictable future under the promise of God.

A final exercise in this context:

✎ Exercise QUESTION FOR HEARERS: What do you think of the challenging sermon? Do you desire this type of sermon? Have you had negative experiences with such sermons? If so, what were they? What form would a challenging sermon have to take in order to convince you?

QUESTION FOR PREACHERS: When did you last preach a challenging sermon (evangelistic or political)? Are you reluctant to preach in a challenging manner? If so, what are the reasons for your reluctance? How might they be overcome?

---

8   H. Gollwitzer, Veränderungen im Diesseits, Mün chen 1973, p. 52f.

94

Chapter 4: The structure of the sermon

If a sermon is to do justice to the hearers, as discussed in the previous chapter, it must have an appropriate structure. In this chapter, we will therefore suggest guidelines for structuring sermons. Sermon should be inviting, well planned and well structured. A preacher who carefully plans and structures their sermons is like an architect and building contractor who build a large house and, in doing so, think with affection of the future residents. They will then enjoy living in the house and do not need to complain about any faults. If we apply this to preaching we can say: Most hearers of sermons would rather follow a diligently prepared sermon than a poorly structured one, and they will be more likely to receive messages and challenges if these are presented in a well structured manner.

The preacher as an architect

However, if we want to understand the effect of a sermon in its entirety we cannot attribute it solely to the preacher's ability. The hearers sense that something takes place in well prepared speaking and attentive listening (i.e. responsible involvement in the success of the sermon) that touches them in their innermost being and moves and changes them. On the other, it may happen that a well-prepared and well-delivered sermon does not produce the desired effect.   The factors involved in the preaching process are so complex that it is impossible to plan the success of a sermon down to the smallest detail.   Yet this will not prevent preachers from working diligently to ensure that their sermons have a good structure. They will desire to improve their skills in this area, because they can assume that it will make their sermons more easily understandable.

I. Invitation to hear

Sermons should not put the hearers off; instead they should invite them as to a feast.   Jesus often used this picture when speaking of his gospel (e.g. Matt. 22:1-10). He wanted to give his hearers a foretaste of the heavenly kingdom, of the joy of God, which people are to experience here on earth. Many preachers put a lot of effort into grasping the full message of the biblical text and considering the theological problems. Nothing seems to be lacking. Yet that which is said cannot easily be received; there is no invitation to hear. The following extract from a sermon on Philippians 4:4 is an example of this:

"The Lord is near! His nearness already affects the life of the Christian in the here and now, and fills it with joy. Therefore the scripture states: Rejoice in the Lord always. The joy that comes from him is not crushed by the cares and problems of our daily lives; it overcomes them. Our often joyless and depressing existence is neither played down nor idealised; it is genuinely changed, just as Jesus Christ gave new meaning to the lives of the people he met while he was on earth."

"Factually correct" is not enough   All that this preacher says is correct. However, they say far too much in just a few sentences. One dogmatic statement is followed by another. Before the hearers are able to receive and consider what the coming of Christ means for them, they are already expected to rejoice about it, and to leave the things that burden them behind, because their lives now have new meaning. How is anyone supposed to follow? The hearers switch off, their minds begin to wander. Preachers should not be surprised that the information they give is not received. The gospel that they want to preach is not a gospel, because it cannot be heard.

1. HEARING SIMPLIFIED

Speeches and texts that are too difficult can be made easier. When it comes to understanding, readers have the key advantage over hearers, that they can read a sentence again. Readers can consult others if they found something difficult to understand and have it explained to them. The hearers of sermons, in contrast, have to understand immediately what they are told. They cannot have it repeated to them.

This is why sermons need to be carefully prepared. In them, the hearers are given known and unknown information. The known information reassures the hearers, the unknown information helps them to understand more. If the sermon contains a lot of unknown information, the hearers must have sufficient time to process it. They need breaks so that they do not grow weary on the road along which the preacher expects them to travel. The hearers need something that will stimulate them, something that will help them to remain attentive or that will catch their attention. This applies to informed and less informed hearers alike. All hearers benefit when they are presented with known information in a new and more appealing way, and with unknown information in a way that they can comprehend it. That is what the term redundancy means in this context. The Latin root of this word is *redundare*, meaning to flow back, to flow around and to overflow. Here it does not mean that which is superfluous, as in other contexts. We do find this kind of redundancy in sermons as **Redundancy** well. It makes them boring. They have nothing to say to the hearers. It is a case of more is not necessarily better.

Usually, however, sermons suffer because the preacher wants to say too much. There is a lack of redundancy, i.e. consolidating repetition. This may be illustrated as follows:

It would be better like this:

Redundancy is as important in a sermon as, for example, in a television news programme.

EXAMPLE: *The news that a train was derailed between Hamburg and Berlin and that a number of passengers were injured in the accident may be expressed in a few factually correct words. However, in order for the hearer to better receive and process this information, the circumstances of the accident must be described in detail. The television news creates this redundancy by inserting a film report after the newscaster has read the news item. The location of the accident is shown with the derailed carriages. Eyewitnesses are interviewed. A spokesperson of the railway company is shown answering questions concerning the accident and how it might have been avoided. All this makes the information redundant. If there is no such redundancy the viewers will switch off, and switch over to another channel. The viewer does not make the effort to evaluate and assess the information. It is no longer of interest to them. They quickly forget what has been heard and seen.*

Variation in form and style
Preachers can glean something from radio which uses the imagination to paint pictures and from television. After all, broadcasters want to arouse the hearers' interest in what they have to say. There are many ways in which this can be done. Some result from attentively studying the biblical text. Others present themselves as a result of the particular preaching situation. Various formal and stylistic elements may be employed when interpreting the biblical text in the sermon. Depending on the scripture, these may include:

- Exact information about a subject matter (Jesus behaved in a completely unexpected way...)

- Important background information (The shepherds were on the fringes of society...)

- Clear explanation of a term (The kingdom of God is not a political entity, but...)

- Brief reference to known facts (Jesus healed the sick ...)

- Directly addressing a particular issue (Many people have trouble with this saying of Jesus...)

- Detailed description of a metaphor (Christ, the light of the world ...)

- Brief comparison (Christians are supposed to be the salt of the earth ...)

- Idiomatic expressions and puns (You scratch my back, I scratch yours ...)

- Narration (from the bible, literature, everyday experience ...)

Of course, there can be too much redundancy. When this is the case, the sermon simply marks time in respect of its content and the hearers get bored. Continual repetition may also be interpreted as an attempt to manipulate, because the hearers are not given room to use their own imagination.

2. NARRATION IN PREACHING

One of the most important tools for structuring a sermon effectively is narration. The preacher unfolds a story to her **The bible** hearers. She tells about something that happened to her or about a **- a story** conversation that has been on her mind over the last few days. **book** Anyone opening the bible will soon discover that it is first and foremost a storybook. The bible tells stories about life, stories about God and the world. These stories speak of things past and things to come, and in both cases they surprise us, time and again, with things related to our day. The biblical stories tell us of hope and despair, of love and failure, of power and of impotence.

Once a scribe came to Jesus and asked him questions. The people standing around him listen in suspense: What answer will Jesus give him? He tells a story of a man who fell into the hands of robbers somewhere in the hills between Jerusalem and Jericho (Lk. 10:30-35). Jesus uses a common occurrence of that day and makes it into a parable by describing the people who pass by. The account of the "Good Samaritan" is one of those biblical stories that become deeply engraved on the mind of anyone who hears them.

Stories can evoke memories and bring long forgotten experiences back to the minds of the hearers and place them in a new light. Stories address deep longings and profound hopes, and raise important questions regarding life. The decisive thing about **Biblical** biblical narratives is that they leave room. Hearers are not tied **narratives** down. They can decide to what extent they want to take part in **leave room** the fate of the various characters, with which of them they want to identify. Have I ever "fallen among thieves"? Have I met a Good

Samaritan in my life? Have I ever left anyone "lying by the way side"? Sometimes it is the small things, the minor characters, the subplots that touch our hearts and show us new ways how we can act and live our lives.

a) Types of narratives - some rules for storytelling

Before we take a closer look at *everyday narratives* and the *retelling of biblical narratives*, we will begin by introducing some types of narratives and a few basic rules for telling stories. Our aim is, firstly, to give an overview of the kinds of narratives available to the preacher and, secondly, to offer some useful guidelines regarding the structure of narratives as a practical help for telling stories.

Examples of narratives include:

The retelling narrative
- The *retelling narrative* follows the basic direction of the biblical text. It is not necessary to recount all the details of the story, but rather to retain the essential elements: the constellation of characters, the places, the turning-points in the story-line.

The summary
- The *summary:* The gospels (Matt. 15:30; John 7:1) and the Book of Acts (8:1) contain reports in which extended periods or a series of events are summarised. Similarly, the preacher may give a brief overview of the fate of an Old Testament prophet or the Passion of Jesus. Thus, it is possible to show connections between events and put individual biblical statements in context.

The background narrative
- The *background narrative* is an attempt to introduce historical background information (e.g. what was the life of a shepherd like in the days of Jesus; why were tax collectors unpopular ...) in the form of a story rather than by way of explanation as in an encyclopaedic article.

- The *context narrative*[1] is also concerned with providing the background to biblical events. All the parables of Jesus and most of the prophetic texts of the Old Testament are responses to some specific question or issue. The didactic texts of the New Testament epistles too can be traced back to real situations and questions which motivated the authors to write them. The context narrative serves to illuminate these issues. **The context narrative**

- In the *perspective narrative*, the narrator assumes the role of one particular individual involved in the story and recounts the events strictly from that individual's point of view. As a result, even very familiar stories get a new slant and can touch us in a new way. The story of the "anointing of Jesus by a sinful woman (Lk. 7:35-50), for example, may be told from the point of view of the woman, of Simon the Pharisee, of a guest at the table, or of Jesus himself; in each case, the hearer will get a different perspective of the story. **The perspective narrative**

- The *extending narrative* is similar to the retelling narrative, but does not stop there. The hearer is invited to think beyond the biblical text, for example, what may have happened to the "rich young ruler" after the shameful defeat he experienced in his conversation with Jesus (Matt. 19:22), or what Zacchaeus may have done the week after "salvation had come to his house" (Lk. 19:9). **The extending narrative**

Important rules for story-telling include:

- *Choosing the appropriate perspective:* Depending on the text and the situation in which the story is told, different persons and perspectives may be chosen. Diverging from the usual can increase the hearers' attentiveness. **Choosing the appropriate character**

- *Creating an arch of suspense*: Every narrative must have an introduction and a conclusion. In between these two sections we find the main section, just like in a school essay. In a **Creating suspense**

---

1 Biblical examples of context narration can be found at the beginning and end of the books of Job and Jonah; in these two books, the "actual" content is

story (like in a novel or a film), the hearer is kept in suspense if important information is withheld for a while and motives are not immediately revealed, and there is an unexpected twist at the end.

Appropriate language

- *Using appropriate language*: The language of narration is characterised by short sentences (as one would speak not as one would write), suitable tenses are the present and the simple past (*then he went*, not *after he had gone*). The use of direct speech (Jesus said: *"Your sins are forgiven"* rather than *They heard Jesus say that her sins were forgiven*) and the active voice makes it easier to follow the story. Embellishing adjectives (huge, beautiful) should be used sparingly and evaluations (good, evil) avoided where possible. A good story must leave some room for the hearers' own interpretations.

Para-phrasing difficult terms

- *Paraphrase difficult terms:* It helps the hearers if the storyteller defines difficult concepts (kingdom of God, judgement, sin, eternity) by means of the action before introducing the term.

Bringing out feelings and motives

- *Bringing out feelings and motives*: Narration speaks to the whole person. Especially the realm of the emotions is affected. Therefore, a good story does not merely present facts, but enables the hearers to learn something about the feelings and motives (questions, worries, fears) of the persons involved.

Arousing curiosity and raising questions

- *Arousing curiosity and raising questions*: God stories are always notable and memorable. They are able to hold our attention and raise questions: What if? How might it continue? What could that mean?

---

surrounded by a narrative context.

- *Not solving unsolvable issues and mysteries*: Many biblical stories are "always-stories", because they address basic human questions (the meaning of life, the origin of suffering in the world), basic conflicts (good vs. evil; prevailing vs. being defeated) or "matters of life" (growing old, saying farewell). A good narrative tries to let the deeper layers of human existence show through the surface of the action. Mysteries, for example in the account of a miracle, should therefore not be explained, but left as they are. The story focuses more on the effects of the mysterious events on the people concerned.

Unsolvable issues and mysteries

b) Retelling of a biblical narrative

It is surprising to see how many preachers fail to make use of the forms that the biblical texts offer them. After the initial scripture reading, say a parable of Jesus or a story of a prophet, they do not return to the story. During the sermon, the text appears merely in a fragmented form as extracts: "in verse 17 it says ..." Thus, the context of the biblical story is lost to a large degree. The vivid material of many biblical texts provides enough stimuli to translate the theological contents into the present situation of the hearer. Experiences with church services for all age groups (often referred to as family services) show that adults too appreciate when they are told biblical stories in a graphic way. Even among adults, many biblical stories are hardly known or completely unknown! Every retelling of a biblical account should basically invite the hearers to pick up the "original" in order to find out for themselves "how the story really went".

Retaining the context of the story

AN EXAMPLE: *The magus (Matt. 2:1-12)*

"I saw two kings. One shortly after the other. It was a day in October when I observed - people call me a wise man - how Saturn was approaching the constellation of Pisces. Jupiter followed in the same direction. For eight months, the two planets travelled side by side. That surely had to mean something. After all, Saturn is the "Eye of God" and Jupiter the "Star of Kings" Three times, they came very close to each other, but when they finally entered into the constellation of Pisces they appeared to

103

melt together into one. They shone throughout the firmament as one single magnificent star. But that was not all! Before the two planets left the constellation, something strange occurred: Mars joined them. So I studied the books and learnt that in this constellation the Messiah was to be born in the land of the Jews. I did not consider for long, before setting out for Judea. The journey was arduous. Often I did not have enough to eat for myself and my camel, and the lodgings were lousy. Sometimes, when I felt especially weary and shattered, I was overcome by doubts whether my journey would be in vain, whether all the talk of a coming Saviour might be nothing more than a religious yearning. But then, one day, in an inn, I met a foreigner who too had observed the signs in the heavens and had interpreted them just as I had. This encounter brought back my confidence and we continued our journey together. To Jerusalem, of course. Where else? Where, other than in a king's palace would a king be born? In Jerusalem, we were shown the way to the Fortress Antonia. It stood right next to the Temple and was built in the style of a civilian castle. A whole legion of soldiers was stationed there. The guards scrutinised us before announcing our visit to Herod.

There he was, the king. He was poor, for he needed a lot of money and many scientific advisors, ladies-in-waiting, and huge armies of mercenaries. They all had to confirm to him, every day, what was really not the truth: that he was great and powerful and irresistible. When I told him that we had come to greet the newborn ruler, he was gripped by tremendous fear. From the mouths of the scribes, however, I learnt that we should have gone to Bethlehem. That is where the Messiah was to be born, according to the prophet Micah. In Bethlehem, I found the other King. He was lying in a manger, and yet he was indescribably rich, for he had no need of a fortified palace. In the simplicity of a stable, God concealed him from the envy of the power-craving. Neither did he need a duvet, for God warmed him by the breath of the animals. He could do without the knowledge of advisors, because God's truth illuminated him. Not even soldiers did he need, because a host of angels protected him in accordance with his heavenly Father's will.

Two kings I saw

One was poor in his riches.

The other was rich in his poverty.

104

To him we gave gold, incense and myrrh.[2]

When preachers retell biblical stories, they do more than just create redundancy. The fact that hearers find it easier to follow a well-told story is merely a side effect. The biblical story is about the message itself, not merely about giving an illustration of an abstract truth! It is to retain this message that the preacher retells the story. The more the need to retell the story can be made plausible to the hearers, the better. The hearer should feel at home in the world of the biblical narrative, to share the feelings of the persons involved, and to identify with what the story claims. In the narrative, an encounter takes place between the hearer and the content of the story. If the hearers allow themselves to be taken by the story it becomes clear, so to speak from the inside, to what extent the message of the narrative concerns them.

Showing the need for narration

Many sermons are perceived by the hearers as too heavy, because they skip the first phase of the invitation to hear and go straight to the reflection and interpretation phase. The sermon then sounds something like this: "What is said about Jesus here means three things to us today: 1.... 2.... 3...." In such sermons, the preacher wants to "teach" the hearers from the very first moment, instead of giving them time to open up. A person who gets involved in a story will quickly be led to the point that the preacher wants to bring across. That is why Jesus told parables. His intention was to confront his hearers with the truth of his person and his message. The truth comes to light. It breaks through, it shines through, as Jesus tells a story.

Stories allow time

This is clearly evident in the parable of the labourers in the vineyard (Matt. 20:1-15). It would be wrong to impose a particular pattern of thought on this parable, for example the concept of our works versus God's mercy. In this story, we are drawn into a concrete scenario. The story ends with a strange question (v.15). The owner of the vineyard asks his grumbling workers whether they are so angry, because he is so generous. This question decides everything. The aim of the parable is not

---

2   Taken from: F.-K. Kurowski, Du redest mit mir, Vol. 2, Berlin 1974.

proclaim the love of God that is above all and available to all; we know that already from the very beginning. It is at this question that I must decide whether I want to entrust myself to the goodness of God that gives what belongs to God even to the poorest and the last, or whether I choose to stand aloof and grumble. The truth of this story cannot be discovered by reflecting on the universal nature of God's mercy, but by trusting this Jesus - preacher and hearers alike - who vouches for the truth of the story with his own life.

By telling us stories from our world, Jesus tells us his own story. By involving us in stories, he involves us in the story of his own life and death. Telling parables is his great art. All of a sudden, the pictures that he paints before the eyes of his hearers become transparent and the truth of his person and his story comes to light. The same way that Jesus uses pictures, comparisons, symbols and gestures in his propagation of the gospel, we can. We will look at this in more detail in chapter 8 of the book.

c) Everyday-life stories

In his parables, Jesus speaks about his world, everyday life and the circumstances of the people. These things are suited for parables of the kingdom of God. The lilies in the field are not merely flowers by the wayside that no one notices; they tell of the robes of King Solomon and preach about God's wonderful provision for me. The tiny mustard seed is as the kingdom of God: at first, it is small, in the end, as a plant, it is big (Mk. 4:30-32).

Like Jesus, preachers can make discoveries in everyday life that are suited for parables concerning the truth of the gospel. **Everyday** Finding suitable stories is not always easy. It is best, of course, if **experience** preachers can use their own discoveries and experiences. These **is suitable** are close to the preacher's heart and can therefore convey them to **for** the hearers in a convincing manner. Suspense is not the decisive **parables** factor. It will only capture the hearers' attention for a little while. If stories are merely a peg on which nothing hangs they will distract the hearers from the actual message. If stories do not touch people in the very depth of their existence they are better omitted altogether.

When we suggest that stories constitute an important element in preaching, we are raising a fundamental question: How will the hearer feature in the propagation of the gospel? How can they be involved in the action so that it becomes easier for them to comprehend the truth? On the other hand, are they still left with enough room to consider what the story means to them, despite being so closely involved?

What a good story or account is capable of achieving can be shown by way of the following simple example taken from the diary of the Swiss writer Max Frisch:[3]

"Today, Ursel, our six-year-old daughter, asked me, in the middle of playing with her toys, whether I liked to die. 'Everyone has to die,' I replied from behind my newspaper, 'but nobody likes to die.' She ponders. 'I like to die!' 'Now?' I asked: 'Really?' - 'Not now, no, not now!' - I lower the newspaper a little so I can see her. She sits at the table, mixing watercolours. 'But later,' she says and draws in silent enjoyment, 'later I will like to die.'"

In this account, experiences that everyone can have, fears and desires that everyone knows, are condensed into one scene. The **Narratives** hearers are left to think about these things. At first, they may **address** reject this issue, but somehow the question of dying will not go **issues** away: Do I like to die? Why do I not want to think about my own **of life** death? What could help me when it's my time to die? - Or a hearer may want to know how they can help a dying relative. Or perhaps they are surprised that a child would ask about death, and wonders what might have triggered the little girl's question.

The preacher's story may sometimes be better than that which they have to say about it later in the sermon, and better than their **Learning** response to any questions that the hearers might ask afterwards. **to tell** The seemingly innocent scene continues to affect the hearers. **stories** This is due to the fact that a well-told story is able to relate to real life and, in doing so, it declares the truth of the gospel. A sermon draws its life from being rooted in the depth of real experience. For this reason, preachers need to learn how to choose and tell suitable stories, whether they be taken from the preacher's own experience or from literature. It is far better to choose something from a collection of stories (of which there are many available, including in electronic form with convenient search functions) for one's sermons than to do without any narration at all, because of a lack of ideas.

Dreams condense experiences In telling stories from the richness of human experience, the preacher is not limited to the consciousness alone. Dreams too are capable of touching the hearers deep inside, as they condense experiences into symbols.[4]

"When I was a child, I often had the same dream. I found myself beyond the streets of our neighbourhood in a field with trees and shrubs. I was playing there. The place seemed somehow familiar, as I could still see people and houses. Suddenly, as I was playing, the pursuer rose up behind me. I call him "the pursuer", because I could not see clearly what he looked like. Did he pounce like a lion? I don't know. Anyway, he roared in a loud voice and chased after me. I tried to escape from him; I stood a good chance. The roaring seemed to die away; but suddenly I was overcome with terror. My feet would not go forward. They remained stuck in the ground, as if they were covered with heavy clay. Therefore I could only move forward slowly and the pursuer was back on my heels. With heavy feet, I fled towards the town. I saw the houses, the people - but they could not help me. Running had not become easier, either. My feet now stuck to the softened Tarmac of the streets. With every step, I had to pull them out again. Behind me was the pursuer. The streets grew narrower and became more and more branched. But then, finally, I saw the safe house in front of me. Out of breath from running, I rang the doorbell. Just before the pursuer could get me the door opened; but I couldn't close it. He pushed against it from outside. So my flight continued, up the stairs.

---

3   M. Frisch, Tagebuch 1946-1949, Frankfurt/Main (1950) 1977, p. 349.
4   The following example is taken from: R. Heue, in: werkstatt predigen 7/74, p. 46f.

Again these heavy feet, like lead. Again these heavy, slow footsteps. The door to our flat stood open. Quickly, I hurried inside. Yet again the pursuer had arrived almost at the same time. I could see his mighty stature behind the opaque glass of the door. The door was still a little ajar. Slowly but surely, he pushed his way into the hallway. I remember - so they told - I often used to scream at this point in my dream.

Then I woke up, covered in sweat. My mother came. The light was on. The doors were shut, everything was fine. It is strange that I later dreamt the same dream, but with a different ending. At the point of greatest need, when the pursuer stood outside the door, slowly pushing it open, I took heart. I stepped aside, let the door go and them leapt into the open maw of the monster. It seemed as if my leap had killed him. The darkness lifted. There was light. I was well, and he was gone. Evidently, everything had turned around. Not I had been devoured, but he. I was alive, but he was dead.

Much later, this dream helped me understand a picture that the Apostle Paul had seen: Death has been swallowed up in victory. Sometimes, I think: When death pursues me, when it stands at the door, wants to break through into my life, will I have the courage to open the door as in the dream? Sometimes I think: Maybe Jesus' experience is repeated in us. Where, oh death, is your victory? Where, oh death, is your sting?"

Any preacher who begins to tell stories in preaching will come to realise how few stories they know that are really suited for a sermon. However, once having begun to discover this valuable resource for structuring sermons, they will become increasingly sensitive in this regard. The preacher will experience their world through different eyes; will listen and read more attentively. They will encounter deep layers of our existence that will unveil to them the mystery of the truth of the gospel in our world. This will be felt in their sermons.

We will conclude this section with another exercise to find out hearers' reactions to the issue of comprehensibility and ✎ **Exercise** redundancy. A difficult passage of a sermon (such as the one at the beginning of this chapter) is read to a group made up of hearers and preachers. The hearers are then requested to answer the following questions:

- What have I remembered?
- What did I not understand?
- Where did I switch off and think about something different?

On the basis of the hearers' reactions, the preachers may now work at giving redundancy to the passage and adding to its linguistic form (narrative, example) in order to facilitate comprehension. A second trial will reveal whether this was successful, and how it was achieved. Usually hearers will reward these efforts by judging the revised passage as being better than the first.

In a similar exercise, a group of people analyse a sermon in its written form, specifically in respect of its comprehensibility and discuss where narrative elements might be added to make it clearer and more vivid. More exercise of this kind can be found in chapter 7.

II. Building plans for sermons

Narration is an important element of sermon structure; it is, so to speak, the crystallisation core. Other creative elements for structuring sermons must be added. These include: factual information, background knowledge, and explanation of terminology. Also references to commonly known facts, a description of a picture, brief comparisons, idiomatic expressions and puns belong to the list creative elements, which can be used at various points in the sermon.

The following sermon building plans are meant to correspond to the different types of hearing described in the previous chapter: the search for meaning in life, for direction, and for help with decisions (cf. Chapter 3). Another structural plan is taken from the psychology of learning. This plan takes up elements from the other models and brings them together into one new concept.

1. WHAT A STRUCTURAL PLAN CAN AND WHAT IT CAN'T DO

Structural plans help the hearer to understand the sermon in a deeper way, to take in what has been said, to consider it further, and to change existing attitudes and behaviour. However, well-structured sermons do have certain disadvantages as well. A structure may put a natural train of thought in a straightjacket or not be appropriate for the given biblical text. Or it may be that the structure is not suitable for the hearers; they may not feel comfortable in a "house" with such a ground plan and would prefer to move out sooner rather than later. **Advantages and disadvantages of structural plans**

If the preacher works together with one or several hearers when preparing the sermon, they can select ground plans together that are suitable for the thoughts presented by the preacher and consider their advantages and disadvantages. The preacher can check the sermon with hearers, even after preaching it. A comparison with the selected structure will reveal any shortcomings. Moreover, the question can be raised once more, whether a different building plan might have been more appropriate for the given text and that particular congregation.

2. RULES FOR STRUCTURING A SERMON

Not every preacher will immediately feel comfortable working with models. Some opportunities and limitations have already been pointed out. The following four points should be considered in practice:

(1) It is rarely possible to develop a precise building plan from the very beginning of the sermon preparation and then to adhere to it.

(2) A model is, first and foremost, a framework for checking an already completed sermon plan. After having produced an initial version, the preacher considers, on the basis of the structural models known to him, how he has planned the sermon. Thus, he checks his draft to see where something is missing and what has to be developed further.

111

(3) The preacher can use the model as a basis to improve her sermon. It can help her

- to formulate and develop the topic more precisely.
- to mark the transitions from one section to another more clearly.
- to summarise the message of the sermon in a conclusion and lead the hearers once more along the route that she has taken with them.

(4) Checking the sermon draft against a structural model will show the preacher whether they may have burdened the hearers with too much information. This is likely to be the case if the sermon is developed around more than three focal points.

In general, we can say: The building plan must agree with the aims of the sermon. If the preacher is not sure about the aim the hearers will find it difficult to follow. S/he should consider, for example, how long it will take to acquaint the hearers with the biblical text. Models 1-3 are particularly suited for expounding and interpreting a text step by step. Now let us look at the models one by one:

3. MODELS FOR STRUCTURING SERMONS
Model 1:
Expanding circles

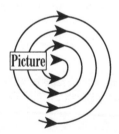

At the centre, there is a picture: the tower of Babel, the good shepherd, the lilies of the field, the mirror image of a woman (cf. example in Chapter 3). With its symbolism, the picture appeals to the depth of our emotions. It is suited for silent reflection; we can take it in, meditate on it. The sermon circles around the picture and does very little interpreting. It encourages the hearers to think about the picture for themselves. The sermon evokes associations rather than following a logical train of thought. The various parts of the sermon are not equally long and equally weighted. They are not closed; the transition from one part to the next is gradual, and the hearers are given room to develop their own thoughts. The preacher keeps leading the hearers back to the picture so they can consider it again and discover something new in it.

Model 2: Perspective structure

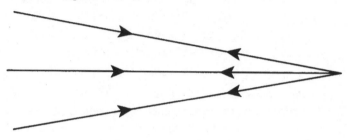

Like model 1, this model belongs to the demonstrative and elevating type of discourse. Model 2 draws a clearer line between the various trains of thought. With one picture as the focal point, the sermon reflects in different directions. The various rays may differ in length and lead back to the picture. Before moving on to the perspective development, the preacher may retell the biblical account.

Model 3: Unfolding structure

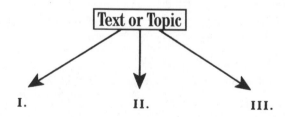

This model is the most well known and most commonly used form of structural plan. It is suited for the informative type of discourse, which appeals mainly to the mind with the intent of giving direction to the hearers regarding particular problems. It has to do with teaching. The layout (plan) facilitates logical progression.

A thematic principle (Example: "Accept one another, then, just as Christ accepted you, in order to bring praise to God." Rom. 15:7) is unfolded in two or three different directions. All the parts are at the same level. They should be equally long as far as possible. At the end of the sermon, the preacher draws a conclusion from the various parts, which is then summarised in a few memorable points. These points may be further reinforced visually by means of an overhead projector or a flip chart.

This kind of visual plan helps the hearer to know which point in the sermon the preacher has reached. If the hearers can assume that the various parts have approximately the same length (and the last one does not turn out to be the longest, because it was not as concisely formulated as the others) then the attentive hearers' patience will not be worn out.

The unfolding model does have its disadvantages. It tempts many preachers to a deductive approach, whereby they make claims without giving reasons ("That's the way it is, believe it!"). The preacher already has his/her topic, instead of developing it in a dialogue with the hearers. The hearers are not given sufficient time to follow critically what is being said. Besides, frequent use of the unfolding model can lead to the hearers getting accustomed to it and bored, especially if they already know that the quality of parts 2 and 3 will not match that of part 1.

Proposed structural plan for a sermon on Matt. 15:21-28 (Jesus' discussion with a Canaanite woman):

Topic: The threefold daring of faith

    I.   Faith as an encounter with the person of Jesus

    II.   Faith as an encounter with the freedom of God

    III.   Faith as an encounter with the future of the world

Model 4: The dialectic structure

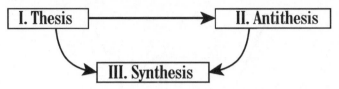

First, a thesis is presented and expounded (Example: "Christians are not better, but they are better off!") Then, an antithesis is proposed against this thesis (Are Christians really better off?). Finally, the preacher tries to make a synthesis by combining the thesis and the antithesis in a forward directed manner. This model is especially suited if the preacher wants to call into question a particular thesis or an aspect of the biblical text, for example in the form of an "anti-sermon" (cf. the example in Chapter 2). This can be done, for example, by referring to individuals (or groups of people) who make such statements ("The other day, my colleague came out with it again: God doesn't exist; he is silent."). This is not about creating the concept of "the enemy". Quite often, the antithesis is present in the hearers or even the preacher themself as a trial of their faith! In the synthesis, the preacher then tries to give answers to the antithesis from the gospel. Thus equiping the hearers with good arguments to counter the antithesis in everyday life or in specific trials. In many cases, however, they will not be able to do much more than encourage the hearers to "believe against the facts". The faith of the hearers is strengthened; with the help of the *dialectic structure* model, the preacher can provide them with arguments to defend themselves against trials and animosity for the sake of their faith.

Proposed structural plan for Matthew 15:21-28:
Topic: The silence of God and the promise of Christ
Thesis: Our attitude towards God: the (false) security of "cheap grace" (Dietrich Bonhoeffer)
Antithesis: The silence of God: his resistance against our security
Synthesis: The power of pleading: Jesus will not leave anyone who cries out for help.

Model 5: Progressive-deepening structure

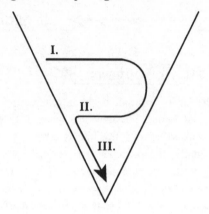

This building plan is suited for both the informative and the challenging type of discourse. The sermon, which again appeals first and foremost to the mind, has a broad and open beginning. Many hearers feel invited. The topic is meant to be interesting; the hearers are invited to think about it. In the two subsequent parts, the sermon goes deeper into the topic. The second part supports the first by giving background information. In the third and final part, the sermon moves on to the core statement. The broad subject of the beginning is continuously narrowed down until a final judgement is reached. The hearer is supposed to agree with this judgement: "That's really the way it is."

Proposed structural plan for Matthew 15:21-28:

Topic: The test of faith

I.   The physical need of the woman and Jesus' harsh rejection

II. Her experience of the limit and the impossibility of help

III. God is overcome and praise from Jesus

The progressive-deepening model is often used in sermons that call for a decision. The hearers may be shown in the first part, for instance, that certain approaches to life (Rom. 2:1ff) will lead them in the wrong direction (legalism). In the second part, the hearers are then shown that salvation is only found in Christ (Acts 4:12). Finally, in the third part, they are directly confronted with this message (2 Cor. 5:20). They are challenged to make a decision for Christ, for life, not death. But what does that actually mean? Many preachers who use the progressive-deepening model find this hard to explain. A simple "Jesus is the answer!" will not do. The preacher must be able to show the hearers how the journey will continue after they have made a decision for a life with Christ. Having been led to the narrow gate, they must now be able to see the open plain, for the call of commitment to Christ opens up the "glorious freedom of the children of God" (Rom. 8:21).

The progressive-deepening model makes it possible for the preacher to "get to the heart" of the issue, to present very different alternatives and, finally, to lead the hearers to the point of decision. However, the preacher should be careful not to adopt a "minus-plus theology" that will hardly appeal to a critical hearer.

Model 6: The learning psychology structure
This structural plan, which is currently receiving a lot of attention in the context of the rediscovery of the sermon as a learning process[5], will be described in greater detail. This structure takes up elements of models 1-5 and develops them further. Model 6 is the result of research into the psychology of learning. It is intended to help the hearers to enjoy listening to the sermon, to follow it critically, and to stay with it to the end by providing them, every now and then, with opportunities to "take a rest". Listening should not be tedious; it must be made easy.
The learning psychology structure comprises five phases:

(1) *Motivation.* In the first phase, the hearer is "picked up" **Motivation** and invited to listen. They should be motivated to listen to the whole sermon right to the end and to open up to the solutions offered at the end. Narratives, dialogues, meditations on pictures, references to current affairs can all serve as tools for motivation. The preacher does not begin by presenting a problem. They do not immediately want to teach the hearers something. Instead, lead them to the message one step at a time. The preacher wants

---

5   Cf. H. Arens, Predigt als Lernprozeß, Munich 1972; P. Bukowski, Predi gt wahrnehmen, 2nd Ed., Neukirchen-Vluyn 1992, p. 31ff.

to get to the place in the lives of the hearers where the problem lies. Doing this very gently and carefully they are approached in a personal way, so as to establish a basis of trust. The message will be received more readily if the preacher manages to build a good relationship with the hearers. This is an important function of the motivation phase.

In chapter 3 (p.85), we have already discussed an example that uses the learning psychology structure. In his radio address, Horst Hirschler spends a lot of time on the motivation phase. He wants to induce his hearers to use their imagination and to think about celebrating Christmas. For this purpose, he tells of a discussion in a church youth group where the young people express their discontent and frustration regarding the Christmas celebrations in their homes. The problem is exemplified by a specific situation. The young people know, like the representative of the older generation that Christmas should be celebrated in a way that conveys the meaning of this Christian feast.

Presenting the problem
(2) *Presenting the issue.* Phase 1 leads to the key question that the preacher wants to address: "In fact, no one really had anything good to say about Christmas, even when I specifically asked them." Hirschler expects a great deal of displeasure on the part of his hearers. This is why he merely names the problem, which is quite sufficient in the given context.

If the motivation phase was successful the preacher should not normally have any difficulty introducing the problem. Having already prepared the hearers for it, they are now able to unveil an issue that concerns the hearers, or confront them with a current problem. This needs to be as precise as possible. The issue must be clearly circumscribed. Any overlap with other problem areas at this point can create disruptive factors that will remain throughout the sermon. The hearers must feel that the preacher is concerned with the problem as well. Preachers do not feel superior to hearers and are searching for solutions together with them. Thus, the relationship between the preacher and the hearers is strengthened. The hearers will now find it easier to occupy themselves with the issue at stake and think about it for themselves.

A useful method for this phase is to consider the experiences, events and stories that served as motivating factors with regard to their subject content and/or the scope of the problem they raised. The problem, which was presented indirectly during the motivation phase, is now named and defined. At this point, the biblical text may come into play. It is introduced or, if it was read before the sermon, taken up once more. The preacher shows how the text relates to the sermon.

In the radio address by Horst Hirschler, there is no reference to scripture. He might have introduced a biblical text as follows: "In fact, no one really had anything good to say about Christmas. Everybody thought that something special should happen when we are to celebrate the birth of Christ properly. At that time, in Bethlehem, there was also a lot going on ..."

(3) *Trial and error.* After having introduced the problem, many preachers immediately offer a solution. As a result, the **Trial and** hearers are often not able to keep up. They are still occupied with **error** the issue that the preacher has just addressed and need more time to think about it. Besides, there are very few problems which have only one possible solution. Some hearers want to be involved in the search for a solution. The preacher can help them by suggesting various possible solutions and going through each of them. If the preacher is convinced that a proposed answer will lead to a dead end, they convey this to the hearers. They expose the error. Or may leave it to the hearers to decide for themselves whether the various attempts to find a solution lead anywhere or not.

The aim of the "trial and error" phase is to enable the hearers to enter into a debate with their own convictions and those of others. The more serious the hearers are about their convictions, the easier they will find this process. The hearers need arguments which they can also use in discussions with their friends, relatives, neighbours, and work colleagues. It helps if the preacher illustrates the arguments by means of examples and stories. This will make it easier for the hearers to listen after the sometimes rather abstract introduction of the problem. It is important in this context that the "trials" introduced in the sermon are taken seriously as trials and are not mere ciphers. An important characteristic of a fair, objective debate is that it treats the very positions that it has to criticise (on the basis of the gospel) with due respect.

The address by Horst Hirschler is convincing in this phase. In the author's opinion, there is no definite recipe for a Christian Christmas celebration. Hirschler makes that clear through a series of questions. However, he does state his own personal opinion that the older and the younger generations should take time to listen to one another at Christmas, and therefore celebrate it together. This is what Hirschler offers as a answer to the problem.

Offering a solution

(4) *Offering a solution.* If the preacher has convinced the hearers in the trial and error phase of the seriousness of the issue and of various trials to find an answer, then the hearer will accept or receive the solution proposed by the preacher more readily. It is here that the biblical text, above all, should be allowed to provide an answer. The perspective of faith is made plausible. The fact that this does not lead to easy remedies, but often to more questions and problems, does not need to be explicitly stated in every sermon; it should, however, be remembered. Answers of faith often raise more issues than they can solve. Although this fact cannot be disregarded, the solution phase seeks to strengthen people in their faith, so that it can give them direction and encourage them to change their behaviour. That leads us to the final phase of this sermon structure: the consolidation of the solution.

In our example, the offer of a solution is formulated rather cautiously. This is in accordance with the nature of the address. However, some hearers will be unsure what is meant by "Jesus' style". At this point, further biblical guidance towards an "Operation Christian Christmas" would be helpful.

(5) Consolidating the solution. When the preacher offers a solution to the problem addressed in the sermon, they should not do this in the form of a general statements ("Anyone who does not ... cannot expect to ...) or appeals to "everyone" ("Everyone should ..."). Instead, there must be specific suggestions that can help the hearers to find solutions to similar problems.

Consolidating the solution

It is essential that the preacher applies their solution to the everyday world of the hearers and presents them with specific, practical steps that they can take. The preacher illustrates by way of examples how they or others might apply the solution in their own lives. He points to experiences that people have had in this regard (cf. the address by H. Hirschler, lines 78-84). Or he may refer back to the example used in the motivation phase. Thus, the question posed at the beginning is answered. New information at this point would interfere with the progression of thought. The purpose of the consolidation phase is to relate the matter at stake to the everyday lives of the hearers. If this is successful the sermon will continue to affect the lives of the hearers and urge them to put it into practice. Generally speaking, anyone who works with models such as the ones discussed above will have to consider what overall direction they want the sermon to take. What is the aim, and how will the hearers be motivated in the direction of that aim? A preacher who is guided primarily by the deficits of the hearers ("I tell you, what you still lack!") must be aware that, for many hearers, he is leading in the direction of a faith that is ultimately motivated by fear. In contrast, a sermon that is guided by the promise of God, by the new life given to us through God's grace and redemption will lead towards a faith that is motivated by fulfilment.

Summary of the learning psychology model follows

Phases	Progression	Aims	Methods
(1) Motivation	1 →	To arouse interest To establish a relationship between the preacher and the hearers To lead the hearers towards the topic (text)	Current examples and experiences Provocative statements Directing thought from the general to the specific and vice versa
(2) Presentation of the problem/issue	2	To establish a relationship between the hearers and the topic (text) The ideal case would be: P = H: Preacher and hearers agree P = T: Preacher and topic (text) agree H = T: Hearers and topic (text) agree	Introducing the hearers to the topic or the biblical text Defining the issue and unfolding the topic (generalising)
(3) Trial and error	3 →	To show the complexity of the issue To reflect on the biblical text To get to know various possible solutions To encourage t he hearers to a critical debate with the (topic) text	Argumentation Illustrations Texts Pictures Symbols
4) Offer of solution	4	To formulate ideas (abstracting) To offer a solution To win the hearers' acceptance of/agreement with the proposed solution	Bringing the biblical message to the point (avoid easy remedies) Formulating key statements or memorable assertion
(5) Consolidation of solution	5 →	To apply the proposed solution to everyday life (relevance) To consolidate what has been said at the experiential level	Accounts of experiences Examples of application

4. LEARNING IN FAITH AND CHANGING ONE'S LIFE

The purpose of preaching God's word is not merely to entertain, inform, or instruct. Although Christian preaching does have the potential to solve human problems (after all, God's saving presence is for "real life"!), this is not its only purpose. The aim of the sermon as God's Word in the form of human words is to produce faith (Rom. 10:17) and change in the life of both the individual and the community (Phil. 2:12f). If a sermon has an impact, then that is a gift of God and cannot be credited to psychological or didactic factors. **Producing faith and changing lives** The differences in our understanding, our personal background and our individual aptitude are too great when it comes to dealing with God's word, whether we be preachers or hearers. Preaching therefore cannot rely on predictable learning content, learning steps, and learning success. It is nonetheless legitimate and advisable, in the preaching of the gospel, to keep the obstacles to understanding to a minimum. This entails ensuring relevance to real life and the questions and issues related to it, and an awareness of lifelong learning (sanctification), that must become evident in practical living. The structural plan models described above are not a guarantee for "success" when it comes to the hearers learning and growing in faith and changing their lives; they can, however, facilitate it. Especially the last model introduced is very convincing. The five steps of the learning psychology model are found already in a similar form in the rhetoric of ancient Greece. They are employed in advertising, in literature, and in filmmaking and television[6]. They provide the basis for many sermons without - we may assume - the preacher consciously orientating him/herself referring to the structure!

One more thing must be remembered for preaching practice: preachers will rarely achieve their "learning aim" through one single sermon. This usually happens in a long process in the

---

6   Many movies follow a pattern like the following: 1. The hero and his task 2. The adversary 3. The clash and the victory 4. The return of the hero 5. The end. This pattern is clearly very similar to that of the classical drama as well as that of the learning psychology model.

course of which several sermons take on a special meaning for the hearer. A text or a topic does not have to be covered conclusively in a single sermon. It may be divided up into several sermons, each with a different thematic focus. This used to be practised a lot in the church, for example, in the catechistic sermons. These were a series of sermons, each of which covered one of the main sections of the catechism (the Ten Commandments; the Creed; the Lord's Prayer; Baptism; Holy Communion; Confession). A similar approach is advisable when dealing with a series of connected biblical texts. If the hearers are invited to a topical series and the preacher is able to convey to them that they will gain something by continually attending, they will probably follow such a limited series with interest. Preachers should endorse this by announcing the topics beforehand. If this is possible, they may take up the topics or texts once more in a mid-week church activity (bible study, youth group, etc.) in order to reinforce them. A spiritual learning process, like any process, requires time. Only repetition can lead to depth and change. It is therefore a good idea to unfold a given topic from different angles. In conclusion, we would like to reiterate that (as we have shown in this chapter) preaching is not merely about imparting knowledge but also about strengthening faith and providing help for decision-making. A good sermon structure can facilitate all of these three aims.

Chapter 5: Delivering the sermon

When asked what they imagine a well-delivered sermon to be like people will usually say:

- The preacher should speak as freely as possible and should make "contact" with the hearers.

- The preacher should speak slowly, audibly, and in an understandable way.

- There should be a healthy mixture of lively presentation and calmness.

The answers to this question will, however, differ significantly: according to their age, background and individual conceptions, the hearers will have quite different expectations of the preacher.

The success of a speech act depends on various factors. These include:

- thorough preparation of the message content

- an expectant attitude towards that which must be done

- an air of "tense concentration" - in the positive sense - to ensure that the sermon holds the attention of the hearers and is not boring

- an appealing, communicative style that stimulates the hearers to think for themselves, that opens up new horizons and invites the hearers to respond

- clear pronunciation, and appropriate body language and facial expression in the given situation.

Many of these factors can and must be learnt if preaching is to remain enjoyable. Others are giftings that one will have to a greater or lesser degree. They must be discovered, developed and shaped or, in some cases, kept in check. In the following, we will discuss some of the factors mentioned that are relevant to successful sermon delivery.

I. The manuscript

Preaching a sermon without a manuscript is a good thing - provided it is well done - because the preacher can focus more on the hearers than constantly having to refer to a manuscript or even keeping their eyes glued to it. However, when a sermon is delivered without any notes, there is always a great danger that the preacher will soon get onto a favourite hobbyhorse. Preachers may also digress, repeat themselves or get carried away in details, with the result that the hearers will lose the thread. In any case, it would be wrong to assume that preaching without notes is a sign of greater faith or trust in God: "A preacher must always know what they are saying, regardless of whether they prepare "in passing" or thoroughly, with a clear purpose in mind. The manuscript is then solely a question of the preachers memory rather than spiritual authority."[7]

There are three main arguments for using a written manuscript:

Clarity (1) Producing a sermon manuscript forces the preacher to structure the message clearly and think it through. Thus, unnecessary repetition and "chatting" from the pulpit can be avoided. Moreover, it will be easier to check and evaluate the results of the preaching process.

Security (2) Having the sermon in a written form gives the preacher sense of security. Even if a preacher is very nervous or has a blackout in the pulpit and does not know how to continue, they can still finish the sermon by referring to the manuscript.

Reusability (3) Finally, a manuscript makes it easier to preach a sermon again. Especially, if the sermon was written on a computer it can always be updated and adapted to the new situation. Thus, a sermon content that was prepared with great diligence can be used with a good conscience on several occasions.

The danger of writing out sermons lies especially in the temptation to read and remain glued to the manuscript. It is also important to be aware of the tendency to use complex "written

---

7   W. Klippert, Vom Text zur Predigt, Wuppertal/Zurich 1995, p. 36.

language" that is likely to overtax the hearers. Adhering to a manuscript can seriously hinder the spontaneity of the sermon. Wolfgang Klippert states in this context: "The manuscript is a servant, not a master. It must not rob its master of the freedom to incorporate current events and new ideas ... A preacher who makes himself the slave of his manuscript will miss the *kairos*, God's perfect timing, in key situations. You should basically follow your manuscript and not try to work in every thought that crosses your mind or even interpret it as the 'leading of the spirit'. You should, however, gladly abandon your manuscript whenever the situation demands it."[8]

In his preaching manual, Horst Hirschler, too, argues in favour of writing out the sermon, but suggests that key words and phrases should then be underlined and highlighted in different colours. The preacher should familiarise him/herself with the prepared manuscript and later, in the pulpit, rephrase every sentence.

We neither consider it necessary nor helpful to memorise the sermon, for a memorised delivery is not a genuine communicative act, but the "reading from an inner manuscript" (Friso Melzer). Besides, there should always be room for discoveries and ideas of the moment, for improvisation and consideration for the hearers. **Memorising** However, in order to effectively use your free leg, you must stand **the sermon** on firm ground with your pivot leg. It is therefore helpful to familiarise oneself with the sermon's structure and the main train of thought.

Roman Catholic theologian Albert Damblon gives plenty of advice on how to get away from depending on manuscripts and become a free - not freely drifting! - preacher. However, he argues against producing a fully formulated manuscript and suggests, instead, the use of notes containing key words and memory aids.

---

8   Ibid., p. 138.

Damblon lists the following arguments in favour of a free sermon delivery:[9]

(1) The free sermon is a public testimony of the message of Christ. The competence to preach includes the ability to "answer to everyone who asks you to give the reason for the hope that you have" (1 Pet. 3:15) freely and convincingly.

(2) Free speech emphasises in a special way the nature of preaching as a testimony of Christ. Someone speaks freely about the things that "really concern us" (Paul Tillich). In biblical terms: "Out of the overflow of the heart the mouth speaks (Matt. 12:34)."

Reasons for preaching (3) Free preaching is "speaking while thinking". This shows: the preacher thinks about what is said not only while preparing the sermon, but also while delivering it. Thus, there is closer correspondence between the speaking process of the preacher and the thinking process of the hearers. Pauses in speaking are pauses in hearing.

(4) The communicative situation of the sermon requires an appropriate form of language, which is not the written word, but the spoken. The latter is more situational, simpler in style, unique, dynamic, provisional; written language, in contrast, tends to be more static and repeatable.

(5) Free speech establishes contact. Even though the sermon is by definition a monologue, it should be a dialogue in character. The preacher has an inner dialogue with their opposite. Preachers therefore need the freedom of speaking, so that hearers can find the freedom to hear.

There are many arguments in favour of free preaching. This, however, requires a considerable presence of mind (as well as the presence of the Spirit!). Like every art, free preaching is both a matter of talent and of diligent practice. Nonetheless, it must be said that free preaching is neither the measure of all things nor everyone's thing. There are good preachers who are experienced in their use of manuscripts and communicate successfully, because

---

9   A. Damblon, Frei Predigen, Düsseldorf 1991, p. 25-46.

they consciously seek contact with the hearers. Under no circumstances should a lack of preparation be the reason for doing without a manuscript. Werner Jetter comments in this context: "the Holy Spirit will not make up the overtime that the preacher tried to get out of doing".[10]

So what should a manuscript look like? A well-tried format is A5. While the preacher may find that A4 sheets are too large for **The** some pulpits, formats smaller than A5 will require turning of the **manuscript** pages too frequently. If there is nowhere to put a manuscript and the preacher can cope with only a few notes they can always resort to A6 index cards. In any case, the sheets should be numbered with writing only on one side, so that the relevant passages can be easily found. To ensure that no lines are skipped or repeated, the writing should not be justified. It is also important to use a large font (or large handwriting), especially in dim light or if the pulpit is quite low. Section headings help the preacher know where has reached in the sermon. The main scripture should, if possible, be read from the bible, not from the manuscript. Thus, it is clear to everyone that the holy scriptures are being cited, and everyone will be able to read the same text again at home in the bible.

II. Contact with the congregation

We have already touched on this in the previous section: preachers should be aware of their congregation. They will notice many things if they watch the hearers. Preachers will sense and see whether they are following the sermon or whether they are elsewhere with their thoughts. The latter, of course, need not always be negative. When hearers allow their minds to wander, this may actually have been triggered by an interesting statement or picture, and sometimes even be desired by the preacher.

We suggest that, while delivering the sermon, the preacher should choose three to five persons within the congregation and **Eye contact** allow his eyes to move calmly from one face to the next. It is always encouraging to see a hearer respond with a friendly smile.

---

10   W. Jetter, Homiletische Akupunktur, Göttingen 1976, p. 106.

129

Moreover, looking at the hearers gives them the feeling that you are talking to them and not over their heads. The worst thing a preacher can do is focus on a fixed point in the church building somewhere above or below the hearers' faces. Thus, the preacher reveals that he is insecure and creates an atmosphere of anonymity. In contrast, eye contact "creates an atmosphere of openness and personal closeness" and "conveys an impression of honesty and self-confidence".[11]

Indications that the hearers have been lost include checking the time or flicking through the songbook or the bible, rustling sweet wrappers, complete absent-mindedness and, in extreme cases, falling asleep in the pew. All these things can be very off-putting for the preacher. Crying children, too, can distract both the preacher and the hearers, regardless of the fact that parents should feel welcome to bring children and their presence in the service is important. In such situations, the preacher may simply repeat a sentence or passage of the sermon without much ado. The same applies, when someone leaves the room during the sermon. Very rarely should this be taken personally and understood as a reaction to the sermon. Usually, there are quite natural reasons ...

Making the congregation laugh
The question of humour will be discussed in a different context in chapter 8. Here, we would simply suggest that there are several reasons why it may be helpful if the preacher succeeds in getting the congregation to smile or laugh. It helps the hearers to relax and take a fresh breath, and wakes them up. Any humorous remarks must, of course, suit the situation and the text. As a rule, one could say it is not a bad idea if the congregation are given at least one occasion to laugh during a church service.

III. The effect of the voice

Accepting one's own voice
"You should accept your voice! ... The mere fact that you accept yourself - including your voice, has such a positive effect on your charisma that you can make a good many points in just a

---

11   W. Klippert, Vom Text zur Predigt, loc. cit., p. 160.

few minutes."[12]   Singers know that a good tone can only be achieved if the person singing is at peace with herself, if there is an inner balance. Insecurity and fear are an obstacle to a good tone of voice and consequently also convincing speech. Now, it is admittedly not easy to accept oneself, nor one's voice, if one is not fond of it. Appeals to accept oneself do not help much in this case. Of more help is the assurance that individuals propagating the good news of the love of God are included in this love. Like everyone else, they are the objects of God's mercy, and therefore they may show mercy to themselves and their voices.

What is important is that the preacher's language sounds as natural and authentic as possible. Put-on emotion and a stilted tone of voice are unconvincing and, after a while, become embarrassing. However, preachers are not usually aware that they do this. It helps to have people in the congregation who give regular feedback regarding this issue (in a loving way!), for it would be wrong, on the other hand, to pay constant attention to one's own voice while preaching. This can lead to excessive self-observation, which will only increase the preacher's insecurity. If the preacher has speech problems that interfere with their preaching considerable improvement can achieve by receiving directed speech training and by working with tape and video recordings of their own sermons.

An adequate volume, clear pronunciation and a consistent pace are, so to speak, the golden rules of neighbourly love, particularly **Volume and** when it comes to people with hearing difficulties. However, this **articulation** rule of adequate volume does not mean that all modulation and lowering of voice should be banned from the pulpit. Some sections must be said quietly or even in a secretive tone to suit the sermon content. Moreover, audibility has to do not only with volume, but also with the precision of speech, i.e. clear articulation. Preachers who do not open their mouths properly, who mumble or slur word endings will not be easily understood even if speaking in a loud voice. If the voice is too low or the

---

12   E. Wagner, Rhetorik in der Christlichen Gemeinde, Stuttgart 1992, p. 314.

speech unclear the hearers suffer, as they have to strain in order to understand what is being said. Consequently, they will grow tired more quickly and "switch off".

The right pace is also very important in preaching. The rule of **Speaking** thumb is that it is always better to speak slowly than fast. The **pace** hearers need time to understand and process what they have heard. For this reason, pausing at the appropriate points is important and helps to underline what has been said. On the other hand, overly long pauses and speaking too slowly can also tire the hearers.

Finally, we need to point out that the hearers too have a responsibility in this area. They can make their contribution to hearing and understanding the sermon, by finding a seat where they can hear well and, if necessary, using a hearing aid or a loop system, and by coming to the service with an expectant attitude.

We do not usually give much thought to the way we breathe. **Breathing** Breathing occurs naturally and subconsciously. However, if we are tense or nervous when preaching we often become short-winded and breathe against the natural rhythm. Breathing too quickly can lead to a disorder of the CO_2 and CA^{++} concentration in the blood which adversely affects our circulation and causes us to become dizzy or may even lead to a black out. This can be avoided by making a conscious effort to breathe slowly in a way that involves not only the chest, but also the belly (diaphragmatic breathing). Thus, the preacher will not run out of breath while preaching. In any case, the breathing determines the syntax. Even if the preacher does not notice when their breathing is inconsistent with the syntax, the hearers surely will.

In churches, microphones or sound systems often do not **Microphones** produce a satisfactory result. If this is the case, one should stress **and** the need to invest in new equipment. It is annoying and disruptive **loudspeakers** when a the hearers have problems understanding, due to poor sound quality, or when a cold, technical reproduction of the preacher's voice lessens the pastoral effect of the words. Just as the acoustics of rooms vary, the effect of microphones and sound systems can vary considerably from one place to another. When being invited to another church as a visiting speaker, it is therefore advisable to check with someone who is familiar with the building how close one should be to the microphone and how loud one should speak, in order to achieve the best possible effect. If possible, the microphone stand or holder should be positioned correctly before the church service. One might also consider whether a microphone is really needed at all. Some speakers limit their elocutionary skills by trusting more in technical aids than in their own vocal ability and charisma. Less technology often means better quality.

IV. Gestures and facial expression

The sermon does not only begin when the preacher is in the pulpit and it does not end when the Amen is pronounced. Our **Body** entire behaviour before, during, and after the service is part of the **language** preaching process. When opening the service, during the scripture readings and prayers, and during the delivery of the sermon, the preacher's manner, like their voice, should be as natural as possible. The preacher should walk to the pulpit upright and at a normal walking pace. Any hectic movements should be avoided. Speaking involves the entire body.

Gestures and facial expressions reiterate the message and lend credibility to that which is said. It is, however, advisable to use gestures sparingly when preaching. You cannot watch a "wriggly" preacher for very long. They make you nervous. Especially movements of the legs and the whole body should be calm. When making gestures, the preacher should look at the congregation. Making gestures to reinforce what you are saying while having your eyes glued to the manuscript usually looks silly. Special attention should be given to the hands. If you don't know what to **Hands** do with them, you can simply rest them on the pulpit. This appears more natural than grasping the edge of the pulpit as if one were trying to find a hold. A person who feels free and steadfast will be able to use gestures in a natural and consistent way. However, the opposite is true as well: moderate movements can have a liberating effect and reduce nervousness.

133

Face By facial expression, we do not mean pulling faces, but looking (in both senses of the word) according to the factual and emotional content. A person who looks bored or distant when delivering the sermon will find it hard to arouse the interest of the hearers. Someone who constantly winks or chews their lips, on the other hand, will pass the nervousness on to the congregation. Again, we are not usually aware of our quirks. There are preachers whose congregations count the times that they clear their throats, take off their spectacles and put them back on again, take a sip of water, or use a particular filler-word during the sermon.

In order to ensure that one uses one's voice, facial expression, and gestures effectively, it is helpful to think of a person one knows in the congregation, to turn to that person inwardly and to speak to them. This helps to make the preacher's manner more natural and personal.

V. Dealing with preaching phobia

There is hardly a homiletics manual that addresses the preaching phobia. Rudolf Bohren writes about the preacher's fear: "The preacher who fears God does not need to fear man."[13] Although this is true, it is probably not all that can be said on this subject.

The most comprehensive discussion on the fear of the preacher is found, again, in Damblon's booklet. He dedicates an entire chapter to this topic. Important findings of his include:

(1) Preaching phobia is normal. Elocution research found that only 8.8% of those tested were not afraid of speaking publicly. The elocutionists Waltraud and Dieter Allhoff state: "Nearly everyone has experienced public speaking phobia: be it in a speech to a large crowd, or an oral exam, or an unpleasant talk with a line manager. Some "have butterflies in their stomach" or "go weak at the knees", others "have a lump in the throat", yet

---

13   R. Bohren, Predigtlehre, 4th Ed., Munich 1980, p 262.

others get sweaty hands, their heart beats faster, or they find it hard to breathe. All these symptoms are not exactly beneficial for speaking."[14]

(2) Preaching phobia must be called by name and acknowledged. On the staircase leading to one pulpit, it says: "Qui ascendit cum timore, is descendit cum honore" - the one who ascends with fear will descend with honour. Thus, preaching phobia is a healthy precondition for preaching, which - provided it does not constantly lead to maladjustments like the psychosomatic reactions described above - contains energy, capable of spurring the preacher to "flight or fight" (i.e. an instinctive maximum performance). The elocutionist Udo Nix states in this regard: "Stage fright is transformed, as spiritual energy, into enthusiasm for the partner and the cause".[15]

(3) The sermon begins with a deep exhalation. Speaking is tonal exhalation. Preachers must therefore control their breathing; stress can easily lead to extreme upper-chest breathing, and ultimately loss of breath. The church father Augustine is quoted as saying: "Breathe in me, O Holy Spirit, that my thoughts may all be holy" - this could also give modern preachers an inner peace that helps to calm their breathing and preaching and allows that which the sermon ultimately wants to achieve to permeate: i.e. to lead the hearers to the Holy.

(4) The congregation is not as critical as you think. What preachers think about their congregation affects the way they preach. Do they perceive the hearers as hungry wolves who are only waiting to tear them to pieces? Or perhaps as innocent lambs expecting tender loving care from their shepherd? Preachers may ask themselves: Are the pews filled only with maliciously intended critics who see themselves as the ultimate authority on preaching and dissect and tear apart any attempt to communicate the gospel? Those preachers should remember that it is the grace of God

---

14 W. and D. Allhoff, Rhetorik und Kommunikation, 6th Ed., Regensburg 1989, p. 60.
15 U. H. Nix, Überzeugend und lebendig reden, Landsberg a. L. 985, cited in A. Damblon, loc. cit., p. 3.

which the congregation has already received long before the preacher ascends to the pulpit. If preachers see the congregation as a community of people who have experienced God's grace and, with that in mind, involve themselves in the communication of the liberating and encouraging message of the gospel, they will want to give to their hearers that for which they so deeply long: namely, a word from God for the here and now, brought to them by a person who hears it personally and endeavours to live their own life accordingly. Bishop Walter Klaiber once asked a pastor who was constantly complaining to him about his congregation: "Do you love your congregation?" A preacher's answer to this question will affect their preaching and the way they deal with preaching phobia.

Love for the church

(5) Thorough preparation. A preacher who is well prepared can depend on their own work. In contrast, a person who lives from hand to mouth will be more likely to fall victim to the stress factor of fear. The rhetorician Maximilian Weller writes in this regard: "First on our list of remedies for inhibitions to speak should be the definite and essential requirement: As a young speaker who is still plagued by public speaking phobia and stage fright, prepare for your topic as diligently as possible, compiling a list of key words, so that you feel you know the topic inside out, that you can produce it 'just like that', and you will be free from insecurity, at least in respect of the subject content."[16]

Thorough preparation

VI. Dealing with mishaps

Many a preacher will have dreamt in the night before the sermon of going into the pulpit and finding that the sermon manuscript has disappeared. Others will have experienced that the sound system failed just as they were about to begin the sermon. Whether the preacher has put on two different coloured socks, the flowers are missing, or unintentional situation comedy (a preacher once announced that he would read a few "verses" from a newspaper article) - such mishaps make a perfect event more

Mishaps make perfection more human

---

16 M. Weller, Das Buch der Redekunst, Munich 1989, p. 67.

human. This applies to church services as well. Thus, mishaps can actually enhance the effect of an event and should therefore not be regarded as something negative. It depends, of course, on the nature and the frequency of the problem. Occasional, minor and therefore non-offensive mishaps rouse a feeling of compassion and empathy in the hearers. Everyone will be relieved and happy when things do finally work out. What is important is that we do not make a drama out of it. Then the mishap is usually quickly forgotten. A little joke relating to the incident may create closeness with the hearers and defuse the situation.

VII. "Advice for a bad speaker"

Kurt Tucholsky, a German author of the early twentieth century, gives the following "advice for a bad speaker". Most preachers will be able to identify at least with some of these humorous and ironical pointers.[17]

"Never begin at the beginning, but always three miles before it! Something like this:

'Ladies and gentlemen! Before I get to tonight's topic, let me briefly ...'

In these few words, you already have just about everything that makes a good beginning: a stiff formal address; the beginning before the beginning; the announcement that you intend to say something, and what you are going to say; and the word "briefly". Thus, you will take the hearts and ears of your audience by storm. For this is what the hearers love: to be burdened with your speech like with a load of school work; that you threaten them with what you will say, what you are saying, and what you have already said. Always keep it nice and complicated.

Do not speak freely - that conveys an impression of uneasiness.

The best thing is to read the speech. That is reliable, and everyone is happy if the reading speaker looks up after every

---

17   Taken from: K. Tucholsky, Gesammelte Werke, Vol. 8, Reinbek 1975, pp. 290-292.

quarter of a sentence in distrust to see if the hearers are all still with him ...

Speak like you write. And I know how you write: in long sentences - the kind in which you, who, having prepared at home, where, irrespective of your children, you have the peace, of which you are so much in need, know exactly what, after countless embedded sub-clauses, the end will be, so that, moving impatiently to and fro in his seat while dreaming, the hearer, as if in a college, where he used to delight so much in sleeping, waits for the end of such a time ... well, I have just given you an example. That's the way you should speak.

Always begin with ancient Rome and always, no matter what your topic may be, provide the historical background to it. This is not only typically German - it is something that all spectacle-wearing people do ...

Do not be concerned whether the waves that proceed from you to the audience wash back to you - that is nothing but frills. Speak irrespective of the effect, of the people, of the air in the room; keep speaking, son. God will reward you for it.

You must put everything in the sub-clauses. Never say, 'taxes are too high.' That would be too simple. Rather as, 'I would like to add briefly to that which I have just said that, in my view, taxes by far exceed ...' That's how it goes.

Ever so often, drink a glass of water to the people - they like to see that.

If you tell a joke laugh before you get to the punch line, so the audience know when to expect it.

A speech is, what else would you imagine, a monologue. After all, there's only one who speaks. Even after fourteen years of public speaking, you don't have to know that speaking publicly is not just a dialogue, but an orchestral piece: there is a silent mass continuously speaking along with you. And you must hear it. No, you don't have to hear it. Just speak, just read, thunder, story-tell.

Following all that I have just said about the technique of public speaking, I want to mention briefly that providing a lot of statistics will always significantly enhance a speech. That has an extremely calming effect and, as everyone is able to remember ten

138

different figures without any trouble, it makes the speech very enjoyable.

Announce that you are coming to the conclusion of your speech long before you get there so that the hearers do not have a heart attack for joy. (Paul Linda once began one of those dreaded wedding speeches with the words: 'I will now finish.') Announce your conclusion and then begin your speech anew, for another half an hour. This may be repeated several times.

You must produce a plan, not just for yourself, you must present it to the audience - that adds spice to the speech.

Never speak for less than an hour and a half, or it isn't really worth starting at all.

When one person is speaking, the others must listen - this is your opportunity! Abuse it ... "

Chapter 6: Checking the sermon

I. Why the sermon needs to be checked

There are two reasons why a manual on preaching needs to include a chapter on checking the sermon. Firstly, preaching involves craftsmanship. Therefore, the sermon, like every piece of work, must undergo a form of inspection so that the author can check its quality. In this chapter, we will suggest some criteria and give some practical tips for carrying out such an inspection. Secondly, there are compelling theological reasons why preachers should consider ways of checking their sermon. In chapter 1, we said that two complementary factors are required to motivate and legitimise a person to preach: the individual must be convinced that they have been called to preach, and must be appointed by the church to this ministry. The appointment by the church gives expression to the fact that preaching is not merely an individual responsibility given to particular people, but that the whole church has a part in the commission to preach. For this reason, the church members have the right to express their thoughts about preaching and to assess it. In this chapter, we will also look at ways how such an assessment may be conducted. Thus, there are two aspects of checking sermons: self-inspection and improvement of the sermon by the preacher at the end of the preparation process, and dealing with feedback from the hearers after the delivery and their involvement in the preaching process. We will begin with the latter.

"Quality assurance"

II. Sermon follow-up discussion and sermon analysis

In his textbook on homiletics, Rudolf Bohren suggests that sermon criticism is not an optional extra or an appendix to the sermon, but an essential element of preaching itself. Thus, it "spells out the Amen to the sermon without which the sermon cannot be concluded."[1]   According to him, sermon criticism

---

1   R. Bohren, Predigtlehre, 4th Ed., Munich 1980, p. 544f.

includes every form of reaction on the part of the hearers - therefore also the absence of any reaction at all.

Uncertainties and questions

To ensure that sermon criticism is not left to chance, sermon follow-up discussions and sermon analyses have long been an integral part of homiletic training. They are regarded as an effective procedure to improve the preaching performance of the trainees. However, despite the fact that these sermon follow-up discussions have become widely accepted, there are still many uncertainties and questions surrounding them. Before looking at the procedure itself, we will therefore need to make some preliminary remarks.

One reason why many people find it difficult to discuss sermons is the immense importance of preaching. In the Protestant tradition, the sermon is perceived to be at the centre of the church service, and the church service at the centre of church life. Thus, there is a lot expectation regarding the sermon, both from the hearers and from the preachers themselves. Against this background, any critical remarks will carry a lot of weight.

Another reason why sermon follow-up discussions touch on a sensitive area is the fact that the sermon being discussed is in fact a confession of faith of the preacher. Thus, it is about something that determines the person deep inside, and consequently the comments made by others about one's own sermon can cause upset. Besides, the analysis of a sermon may reveal psychological strengths or weaknesses of the preacher. As the sermon follow-up discussion has this potential, it is used in the training of pastors and counselors for the purpose of developing the trainees' personality. In the course of the training, the candidates learn to perceive themselves and others more consciously. The candidates' personal and communicative competence is increased; however, this often involves a painful process of getting to know oneself.

One question that is asked time and again by members of the congregation in the context of discussing sermons is whether it is right to criticise a sermon, as it is (or at least contains) the Word of God. Does this not put the Word of God in danger of being compromised? Our response to this concern is that sermon follow-up discussions have the exact opposite aim: In preaching, God's Word always goes out in the form of human words - with all their shortcomings. These human words need to be examined so that the message will come through all the more clearly. Thus, it is not the Word of God that is held up for criticism; on the contrary, the aim is to make it as perceptible as possible. Yet we must also warn of the danger that sermons can be "flogged to death", especially if they are discussed with an unloving attitude. It is therefore important to know something about the function and methodology of the sermon follow-up discussion.

In sermon criticism, we can distinguish three basic areas, although they are all in some way closely related:

(1) First, there is the theological dimension. "Test everything. Hold on to the good." (1 Thess. 5:21) The source and the **Theological** measure of all that is said in the Christian church in the name of **dimension** God is the gospel of the triune God's love for humanity as testified to us in the biblical writings. Every sermon should be measured by this standard.

(2) Next to the theological dimension, there is an **Anthro-** anthropological dimension. Our preaching must orientate itself to **pological** the respective hearers with their reality of life, their ideas, their **dimension** problems, etc. if it is to reach them. We must therefore check whether the sermon meets the relevant requirements.

(3) Thirdly and finally, we must consider the rhetorical dimension. From this perspective, the sermon is examined to **Rhetorical** determine whether the best possible means of presentation are **dimension** being employed or whether the form in which it is delivered might prevent it from achieving its own aims. In this context, we must give non-verbal as well as verbal signals.

The benefits of sermon criticism are obvious: The preacher should learn to preach better or, more precisely, to satisfy the three criteria mentioned above to a greater extent. Sermon follow-up discussions and sermon analyses provide you with an opportunity to obtain a response to your sermons. To ensure that this "echo" does not die away without being utilised, you must, however, be willing to accept negative as well as positive feedback. Criticism and correction are always better than no feedback at all, provided they are expressed in an appropriate manner. The absence of any reactions can, in the long run, have a very discouraging and paralysing effect.

The post-sermon discussion benefits not only preachers, but also hearers. Hearers who know that the sermon will later be discussed are bound to listen more keenly and expectantly. In the discussion and the analysis, the members of the congregation take on responsibility for the preaching in their church and contribute towards improving the communication between preachers and hearers. If an opportunity to exchange of views is given, criticism does not have to remain under the surface, where it usually has a destructive effect. Moreover, sermon follow-up discussions provide a good framework for communication between young and elderly, or conservative and progressive church members. Thus, discussions about sermons can help with church building. What is important in the sermon follow-up discussion and sermon analysis is that the hearers do not regard themselves primarily as a commission of experts, but as the addressees of the good news of God with mankind.[2]

Finally, the sermon follow-up discussion is of benefit to the sermon itself, for all sermon criticism serves as an aid for interpreting and understanding the sermon. "It underlines the message of the sermon and broadens its language".[3] It is therefore

---

2   From a theological perspective, this does not prevent a critical examination of the sermon. It does, however, affect the choice of language: "We cannot tell the gospel of the love of God and, at the same time, speak a language that does not benefit those whom we are addressing. That does not mean that a language that loves people needs to sweep everything under the carpet. It is, however, a language that does not regard uncovering faults and accusing those responsible as the greatest cultural and religious merit." (H. Weder, "Die Entdeckung des Glaubens im Neuen Testament", in: Glauben heute. Christ werden – Christ bleiben, ed. by Kirchenamt der EKD, Gütersloh 1988, p. 63.)

3   R. Bohren, loc. cit. p. 545.

worthwhile to work further on the delivered and discussed sermon in order to process and incorporate the criticism that was expressed.

In addition to the aforementioned problems associated with sermon follow-up discussions, there are other problem areas that must be considered before carrying out such discussions:

Most preachers are easily offended if their sermons are criticised. Besides the high level of identification with the sermon, this sensitivity results from the fact that the preacher has exerted themselves, have "given something of themself". When preachers feel attacked or misunderstood, they often try to defend themselves against these emotional blows with theological arguments. If there is no intervention at this point, the discussion dries up or turns into an unfruitful debate on principles.

The preacher's iden- tification with the sermon

It is not easy for the hearers, especially at the beginning of the discussion, to articulate their own impressions of a sermon they have heard. Between being spoken to and conveying what one has heard in the sermon follow-up discussion, a "processing" of one's own reaction may sneak in for several reasons.[4] For this reason, friends and church members will often try to protect the preacher from negative assessments. This can lead to the development of "front lines" between different positions, which make a construct- ive discussion difficult. Similarly, personal dislikes or rivalries, differences in theological positions, or arguments about internal church issues can hinder a sermon follow-up discussion. Any statements in these regards should, as far as possible, be addressed and dealt with in the group; in fact, any discord should be addressed immediately and directly, in order to prevent it from continuing under the surface and having a negative effect on the discussion.

Processing one's own reaction

In sermon follow-up discussions within the church, theological "lay people" often feel inferior to theologians. This can result in the church members remaining silent or "fighting" for a particular

A question of power

---

4 By "processing", we mean the fact that emotions and spontaneous ideas are often first subconsciously filtered and changed before being related in a group setting.

view that has been voiced. It is therefore always necessary to pay close attention to the power issue.

As our church services usually demand a lot of attentiveness of the congregation, it is usually difficult to get them to concentrate again after the service. Besides, some members of the congregation also fear that the sermon might be "flogged to death" and, as a result, they might be robbed of any positive impulses and emotions.

Limitations of the procedure

Finally, we must be aware that the methods of the sermon follow-up discussion and the sermon analysis can only ever deal with certain aspects of a sermon's effect, a realisation that will relieve especially the preachers. The preachers will never be in control of the effects of their own words or of the living dynamic of the biblical texts, which they can neither guarantee nor prevent. The mystery of faith cannot be fully unravelled. Furthermore, it is necessary to point out in this context that there may be an inner opposition to the Word of God in the hearers, which results from the expectations and the offence of the message of the gospel itself and not from the inadequacy of the preacher.

Although fortunately not all the problems mentioned will normally occur in every sermon follow-up discussion, those that lead such discussions should at least be aware of them. Thus far, we have used the terms sermon, follow-up, discussion and sermon analysis synonymously. In the following, we will introduce these two procedures separately.

1. THE SERMON FOLLOW-UP DISCUSSION

a) The purpose

The hearers as equal partners

Experience shows that it is usually easier to say something about a sermon if the discussion begins at the emotional level rather than the cognitive mind-level. Through methods of emotional feedback, the hearers learn in the sermon follow-up discussion to concentrate on the given sermon, to articulate any personal impressions, and to avoid resorting to unfruitful debates on principles. As the sermon follow-up discussion is not a theoretical theological debate, persons with theological qualifications and so-called lay people can take part in it as largely equal partners. Thus, the "priesthood of all saints" and the responsibility of the church are made evident and can be experienced. Yet, it is not enough to find out how people feel about a particular sermon; the discussion should also bring to light what in the sermon triggered these impressions and feelings. As a result, theological and linguistic strengths and weaknesses will become evident. For this reason, the sermon follow-up discussion with its focus on the emotions cannot substitute the sermon analysis, which looks more specifically at the interpretation of the biblical text, doctrinal statements, the ethics of the sermon, etc. As the sermon follow-up discussion and the sermon analysis focus on different dimensions of the sermon, their results may well differ and even be mutually corrective.

b) Conducting the discussion

After the service, the participants in the discussion meet after a short break. Agreeable conditions, such as comfortable seating and an appropriately sized room (with adequate heating in winter!) help the discussion.

The sermon follow-up discussion should, if possible, not be led by the preacher themself. They are too emotionally involved. Sometimes "vigorous moderation" (Hans van der Geest) will be required, which can be accomplished better by someone who is not so personally affected.

At the start, the participants should be briefed on the aim and the methods of the sermon follow-up discussion. Next, the hearers are prompted by means of directed questions to share their impressions with the group. Such questions may include:

Directed questions

- What made a positive impression on me? What bothered me about the sermon? What was the aim of the sermon?
- Or: What message did the preacher convey to me? How did I experience the sermon and the preacher?
- Or: What in the sermon was important to me? What would I like to discuss with the preacher?

Recording feedback

All the contributions of the participants are recorded on overhead projector or a flipchart and put in order. It is important that the hearers talk about their experience of the sermon in the first person (I found ...) so that the preacher is able to accept what they say as personal statements. General judgements should be avoided. All the participants' assessments should be directed towards the moderator. This helps to objectify them, and consequently protects the preacher from criticism that may be perceived as too personal or too harsh. If the same assessment is given more than once, this should be indicated (for example by underlining it) as it is important to distinguish between majority and minority assessments. Any contributions that deviate from the general view should be taken seriously. Minorities need to be protected. During this phase, the group members should not yet comment on the statements of others, except if these statements are obviously not authentic but processed (as discussed above) or they need to be clarified. After the hearers have responded to the questions, the preacher should be given the opportunity to state how they experienced the sermon.

Gathering - not evaluating

This non-evaluative feedback phase of the sermon follow-up discussion should last no longer than 20 to 30 minutes, to ensure that there is still time for the participants to enter into a discussion with the preacher and with each other. It can be an enriching experience if the hearers and the preacher expand on the message of the sermon from their own perspectives, thus helping to go deeper and to make God's Word more topical.

Towards the end of the sermon follow-up discussion, the moderator should try to summarise briefly the course of the sharing of thoughts. This can help to qualify any harsh or even offensive statements of individual and thus, to protect the preacher.

Closing with a prayer or blessing

It is advisable to close with a prayer or a blessing to remind everyone of the spiritual purpose of the sermon follow-up discussion and of the fact that it is still a part of the church service. This spiritual conclusion should, however, not be abused as a means for creating a false sense of harmony.

148

2. THE SERMON ANALYSIS

a) The purpose

In the sermon analysis, the sermon is evaluated in respect of the three dimensions discussed above: i.e. its theological quality, its relevance to the congregation and its communicative effect. During the analysis, great care must be taken not to carry out arguments about emotional issues in the guise of a theological debate, as if they did not personally affect one.

b) Conducting the sermon analysis

As this form of sermon evaluation is more theologically orientated, the sermon analysis is used primarily in the context of preacher training and development or with a limited group of interested church members who regularly discuss sermons. All participants receive a copy of the written sermon manuscript (sometimes with notes from the preparation phase).

(1) A good way of beginning the sermon analysis is by asking **Directed** how the sermon relates to the biblical text.   **questions**

- Which parts of the text does the sermon take up, which parts does it leave out?
- Does the sermon convey the structure and the essential content of the text?
- How is the text applied to the here and now?

In this context, it is important that the sermon is not "buried" by the participants, so they can exalt their own theological views.

Next, the systematic theological considerations and decision in the sermon are examined.

- What kind of God is the preacher propagating? What does God do in the sermon?
- How does the theology of the sermon relate to the scriptures as a whole and to the doctrines of the church?
- Are the hearers perceived and taken seriously, in the sense of the biblical doctrine, as the addressees and the bearers of God's promises?

149

- How does the sermon combine comforting and demanding elements?

The so-called "Heidelberg method" of sermon analysis stresses the significance of the preaching language in this area. It is suggested, for instance, that the frequent use of conditional verb forms and clauses and of modal verbs (may, must, can, etc. + infinitive) indicates a normally subconscious and unintentional legalistic attitude underlying the sermon. "Where the language is not right, the theology is usually not right either ..."[5]

(2) When the sermon is evaluated from an anthropological perspective, the questions focus on the social environment, the specific life situation and the thoughts and ideas of the hearers (and preachers!). Directed questions may be included:

- How does the preacher relate to the hearer?
- Is the sermon content relevant to the hearers, in other words, do they find their situation in the sermon, are their fears, hopes, and doubts addressed?
- "Does the sermon leave the hearers with something to laugh about or to fear" (Rudolf Bohren) or to believe?
- Does the sermon help the hearers to live?
- Does the sermon encourage critical social and political awareness?
- Does the sermon open the door to freedom and future, or does it have a restraining effect?
- Does the sermon have a church building effect?
- Does the sermon bring amazement to the hearers, or does it bore them by merely citing theological facts?
- Can it set something in motion in the hearers?

The anthropological evaluation includes questions regarding the person of the preacher:

- How does she involve herself in the preaching process?
- What does she dare?

---

5   G. Debus et al., "Thesen zur Predigtanalyse" in: Die Predigtanalyse als Weg zur Predigt, ed. by R. Bohren and K.-P. Jörns, Tübingen 1989, pp. 55-61.

- Does she come across as genuine, original, and credible?

(3) The evaluation of the communicative and rhetorical dimension of the sermon looks at the linguistic means that the preacher employed in dealing with the text, the homiletic situation, and the hearers. Possible questions in this area include:

- Is the sermon comprehensible?
- Does the sermon appear focused or confused?
- Does it have a recognisable structure?
- Does the language match the content?
- Are the hearers overburdened with an abundance of information and definitions? Or are they bored with banalities?
- Are the sentences short and concise?
- Are the examples, metaphors, and symbols appropriate, or do they raise undesirable images and confuse the hearers?
- Is the sermon a speech rather than a piece of writing? Is it read or delivered freely?
- Are the facial expressions, gestures and tone of voice in accordance with the content and the person?
- How does the sermon deal with the beliefs and opinions of others? Does the preacher show solidarity with the hearers, or does s/he know everything better?
- How does the sermon relate to the other elements of the service and to its position in the church year?

These questions reveal how closely the three dimensions are related; during the analysis, questions from different areas may therefore be combined. It does not make sense to ask all the questions every time. Rather, one should limit the discussion to those questions that are most relevant to the given sermon.

III. Where two or three ...

Seeing that our sermons are faced with so many questions and criteria, we could easily become discouraged. When analysing sermons in a group setting one will soon come to the realisation that no preacher can please everyone. Often, the very same statement that is perceived by one person as encouraging and

No preacher can (or must) get everything right

151

helpful is regarded by another as nothing but hollow words. This is precisely why it is important to discuss the sermon: so that preachers can develop an understanding of what their words can effect and trigger. On the other hand, the discussion provides everyone who wants to contribute with an opportunity to do so, so that the whole community of believers share the responsibility for preaching. In such a discussion group that is concerned with improving the preaching and thus the understanding of the gospel the presence of God is guaranteed, for here too the promise applies: "... where two or three come together in my name, there am I with them." (Matt. 18:20)

IV. Checking one's own sermon

It is the responsibility of preachers - before they step into the pulpit - to subject their sermons to thorough inspection. For this **Improving** purpose, we will elaborate on some of the questions which have **communi-** already been proposed in the previous section for the sermon **cation** analysis, but which preachers can also put to themselves, and give some additional criteria and tips that will help the preacher to check their sermon. Even though some of the advice we will give may appear self-evident, studies of sermons show that the problems hindering the communication of the sermon tend to be very similar.

1. BEGINNNING AND CONCLUSION

The first step is always the most difficult. Surveys have revealed that the opening sentences usually decide whether the **The opening** hearers will follow the sermon with interest or not. Manfred **sentence** Josuttis formulated an important rule regarding this issue: "The opening sentence should always be short. At that point, the hearer's attention must still be captured; he must be focused on the beginning of the sermon, and on the style of preaching. He can only do this if short sentences at the beginning make it easy for him to follow."[6] He adds: "The first sentence should, as far as possible, be left open in respect of content. This means: It should stimulate the hearer to continue listening, it should cause the hearer become curious, to wonder, to think." In order to achieve this, the preacher may begin the sermon, for example, by referring to an unusual and surprising sentence or thought in the biblical text, or by reading an interesting quote, a poem, or a story. It is a bad idea, on the other hand, to begin by telling the hearers about the problems you have with the text. A person who begins with a negation it is often no longer able to formulate the positive; moreover, the congregation may not expect much of the text and the sermon after such an introduction. A good way of helping the hearers at the start of the sermon is to lead them to the biblical text by way of an interesting introduction. This will make the congregation more receptive to the text.

The conclusion, too, requires some thought. It can remain with the hearers for a long time, especially if the sermon is followed by a period of silence and not immediately by a hymn or prayer. Like in the opening section, it is advisable to use short, concise **The** sentences in the conclusion, but also a quote, a poem, or words **conclusion** from a hymn that reiterate the main thought of the sermon can be effective. The last words of the sermon should not overtax the hearers; this may be the case if they are challenged by the preacher to take a particular action and then left to get on with it. This can be avoided if the ethical impulse for the action is addressed in the middle part of the sermon and well supported with arguments, and the sermon closes with an encouraging, liberating statement that motivates the hearers to action. What is important is to find an end and to have the courage to leave all the important things that could have been said for the next sermon.

2. THE DIFFERENCE BETWEEN SPOKEN AND WRITTEN LANGUAGE

At school we learn by means of literary texts and our own compositions how to express ourselves in writing. Those who go on to higher education learn the principles of academic writing. We later apply all these rules and skills that we have acquired through hard

---

6   Rhetorik und Theologie in der Predigtarbeit, Munich 1985, p.167.

work - be it consciously or subconsciously - when we write sermons. We compose a sermon manuscript. In doing so, however, we must be aware of the fact that such a written text is not yet a sermon. A sermon is spoken not written language, it may not even be a well-rounded speech with clever wordings that can really only be understood when read. What does that mean for the style of the sermon?

The sermon as spoken language

Here, the same rule applies as for the beginning and the conclusion: long sentences should, as far as possible, be avoided. They make the sermon ponderous and difficult to understand. Of course, stress plays an important part in facilitating understanding, too. However, as the hearers do not have the opportunity - as with written texts - to recapitulate by reading a passage over again, the readiness to listen should not be put to the test by the use of embedded sub-clauses. A golden rule from homiletics for radio sermons, where comprehensibility is of paramount importance, states than no sentence should have more than 13 words.

In preaching, it is necessary to have a certain amount of redundancy (cf. chapter 4). The preacher should approach the text or topic from several angles. While the repetitive use of a particular word or expression may be considered poor style in a school essay, it is actually required in a sermon for the sake of comprehensibility.

The importance of a good sermon structure has already been stressed in chapter 4. When carrying out the final inspection of the manuscript, the preacher should check whether the various parts of the sermon are more or less equally weighted and whether the transition from one part to the next is plausible. Mental leaps should be avoided.

Narration is easier to understand than abstract language. For the sermon, this means that the nominalisation of verbs (the recognition of, the accomplishment of ...), which is common in academic writing, should be avoided where possible. Speaking of grammar: the excessive use of passive structures (it has been observed) and conditional clauses (if these words were taken to heart) take away from the substance and credibility of the message. This may also be the case if the sermon contains too many questions that are not answered in the sermon or to which there is no answer at all.

One linguistic issue in preaching that has not yet been resolved is the use of inclusive language. In our experience, many women feel more appreciated if the preacher makes a conscious effort to address men and women alike. Unfortunately, the use of inclusive language can hinder the flow of the sermon. So far, no commonly accepted rule has been found.

Inclusive language

3. LANGUAGE AND CONTENT

As we have already pointed out on several occasions, the preacher should not use religious insider language or the "language of Canaan". If we claim that our church services are public events to which anyone is welcome (cf. chapter 1) and if we want to reach people through our sermons, then we must make an effort to be understood by as many people as possible, both inside and outside the limits of church. If we want our hearers to understand what we are saying we have to speak their language. In order to learn this language, we must listen to what they say and how they say it. This is not to say that the preacher may only use words that are common in everyday language. The Good News is not a common everyday thing. Nonetheless, in preaching it is important to make sure that the language used (like the content) fits the situation of the hearers and does not "talk round it". In this context, however, we cannot ignore the fact that not only do many preachers have a "language of Canaan", but many hearers also have "Canaanite ears", that means "hearer preconceptions and established hearing customs, which develop a remarkable ability in the hearers to hear things differently. We may then rattle on in any language, be it Jebusite or Philistine, Apocalyptic or Existentialist - in the ears of many, it will always become Canaanite; and after we have deducted that which is lost through

Everyday language

spiritual incomprehensibility, we are left with precisely what the previous vicar always used to say."[7]

No common- places
The sermon should always be checked for commonplaces, i.e. statements about *modern man, society, the political situation* intended to include every hearer and to appeal to everyone. Yet, precisely for this reason, they are of no real concern to anyone. Matters are more complex than such generalisations would suggest. "The pitfall of commonplaces lies in the fact ... that they are so inviting, yet when we set foot there, they will not hold."[8] In concrete cases, they do not apply.

There are also theological commonplaces. While being dogmatically correct, their general nature makes them too non-committal and consequently hearers, who have heard them time and again, tend to switch off. If the familiar is not sometimes introduced in a new, unconventional way the sermon may be boring and dry. There is still another problem associated with commonplaces: statements such as "We all know ..." make general assumptions about the hearer. Do we really all know, or is it that some preachers want to know everything better, or do the members of the congregation perhaps know some thing better than the preacher?

Pictures, examples and objects
The use of metaphors, examples and symbolic objects make the language of the sermon more vivid and thus more accessible. More will be said in this regard in chapters 7 and 8. When checking their own sermons, preachers must ensure that metaphors, examples and symbols are appropriate and that they do not raise the wrong images. The same rule applies to the use of quotes in the sermon. They can make a stronger impression on the hearers than the biblical text on which the sermon is based. The author of a quote should only be named if it is really significant for the sermon. Mentioning unfamiliar names confuses the hearers or gives them the feeling that they do not know something that

---

7   W. Jetter, "Die Predigt als Gespräch mit dem Hörer" in: A. Beutel/V. Drehsen/H.-M. Müller (Ed.), Homiletisches Lesebuch, Tübingen 1989, pp.206-221; p.214.

156

they really ought to know. It is something quite different to mention well-known names like Dietrich Bonhoeffer or Martin Luther King Jr. in order to conjure up particular images. This **Miranda** phenomenon can be described with terms miranda and **and anti-** antimiranda. "Miranda means an emotive word that is perceived **miranda** as positive, antimiranda, one that is perceived as negative."[9] Not only individuals, but also place names and particular terms can have an emotive content (e.g. Chernobyl; Ground Zero; Greenpeace). The effect of these words of course depends very much on the respective receivers. Something that is a miranda to young people in the city may actually be an antimiranda to elderly people living in the country, and vice versa.

In conclusion, we can say that many preachers have the problem of wanting to "pack" too much into the sermon. **Less is** However, less may well be more. This principle applies in respect **often more** of number of thoughts, impulses and ideas contained in the sermon as well as to its actual length. Concentrating on a few main points helps the hearers to understand and remember the sermon better. This should also be considered during the final inspection of the manuscript or the notes.

The following "catalogue of virtues" is intended as a checklist for preachers. The humorous nature of some of the points shows the intention that the catalogue should be read with a sense of humour and that, regardless of the diligence required and the responsibility involved, preaching should always remain a joy. After all, nothing is perfect on this earth, not even sermon criticism!

V. Catalogue of virtues for preachers[10]

- I have avoided long, complex sentence structures. I have shortened every sentence that was longer than two lines.
- I have limited the content to two to three main thoughts. I have expounded on these thoughts in a clear and determined way.

---

8   R. Bohren, Predigtlehre, loc. cit. p. 408.
9   P. Bukowski, Predigt wahrnehmen, loc. cit., p. 86.
10 Based on: C. D. Hinnenberg, "Tugendkatalog für Pr ediger" in: Deutsches Pfarrerblatt 75 (1975), p. 297.

- I have chosen the hymns, readings and prayers for the service to match the sermon.
- I have eliminated the language of Canaan.
- I have avoided announcements ("This means: ..."; "I also believe that ...") where they are inappropriate and make the language sound "official".
- I have examined the text with a view to detecting any false emotiveness, always bearing in mind my role as a preacher.
- I was cautious regarding the use of modal verbs (*should, can, must, may*) and changed passive structures into active ones.
- I have avoided participles and nominalisations where possible. Instead, I trust in the verb's ability to convey the message of the sentence.
- I have limited definitive statements ("That's the way it is!") to a minimum.
- I have used conditionals sparingly and purposefully.
- I have avoided successions of sub-clauses (that..., that...). After all, I know: The main thought belongs in the main clause. That's why I have used short sentences.
- As I am not yet able to preach freely (without a manuscript), I have tried to transform my text as much as possible from "written" to "spoken".
- I have made a determined effort not to use clichés. Like commonplaces, they look good on the outside, but are hollow on the inside.
- Unnecessary emphases ("a real conversation") do not feature in my sermon.
- I have checked my metaphors in relation to their meaning and appropriateness.
- I have replaced words ending in *-tion/-sion* with verbs.
- I have broken the habit of portraying things in black and white. Things are more complex than that.
- Complaining kills creativity. I have deleted it from my vocabulary.
- I choose to keep my seminary mode and theological correctness to myself.

- I have used sound arguments instead of well-meant assertions.
- When I discovered abstract statements I asked myself: What for? What next? This helped me to be more concrete.
- Regarding communication, I know: Confrontation gets me nowhere, when trying to win others over.
- Fierce polemic and simplification will only upset serious, dedicated hearers.
- I have considered the image of the churchgoer and worked at trying to improve it.   Churchgoers are not as bad as their reputation.
- I have sought to show solidarity with my hearers, however, without forcing myself on them (false "we").
- Unanswered questions make the hearers get frustrated. That's why I don't ask them.
- I have neither overtaxed nor bored my hearers by the amount and density of information with which I have presented them.
- I have not merely interpreted the text, but given the congregation words of encouragement.
- I did not get bogged down with negatives. I have proclaimed the positive, the genuine opportunity and reality of the gospel.

Part C: Consolidation: The Sermon as Communication of the Gospel

Chapter 7:
The sermon as a communicative event

I. The sermon in the light of communication studies

"Why does man have two ears and one tongue?"

"So that he will listen with two ears and speak with one tongue, not the other way round."

This Eastern saying expresses something that we experience in our daily lives: hearing and understanding, speaking and communicating are part of our daily lives, and they may be successful and or not so successful. Now, what applies to our interpersonal relationships will surely also apply to communication about the bible and the Christian faith.

Throughout the history of homiletic research there have been various "alliances" with other non-related academic disciplines; the dialogue with communication studies, for example, has given a variety of impulses to the subject of homiletics. These impulses will now be discussed:

We will begin with a discussion of the term "communication of the gospel" and then go on to look at some findings of communication research. Finally, we will determine what the consequences these findings have for the way the gospel is proclaimed in the church service and the sermon.

1. A BUZZ WORD - WHAT DOES THE TERM "COMMUNICATION" ACTUALLY MEAN?

In most areas of public life, the word "communication" is used today, be it in the mass media, in politics, in culture and sports and even in our everyday conversations. The word originates from the Latin root *communicare* meaning "to declare, to talk (to someone), to confer". It was not until the twentieth century that

161

Communi-cation is part of being the word entered into our everyday language. One thing became clear: communication is a basic human phenomenon, a "universal condition of being human", as the philosopher Karl Jaspers expressed it. "All that we are," he is able to say, "we are in communication."[1] In today's multifarious use of the term, we can identify a twofold direction of communication:

Receiving

- on the one hand, the object of communication is to understand (i.e. to *receive* something, namely the content of the declaration or the message)

Giving

- on the other hand, the object of communication is to declare something to others (i.e. to *give* or *share* something, e.g. the content of a text)

Understanding and declaring determine our interpersonal communication. We are constantly in the process of sorting and interpreting the countless signals and messages with which we are inundated. We interpret what "reaches" us and pass on to others that which we have understood and which has become important to us.

Understanding and declaring are particularly essential when it comes to communicating biblical contents that have been handed down to us as testimonies from a past era of people's experiences with God. Thus, the continuous process of understanding and declaring also determines how we prepare and preach our sermons. With regard to the aspect of understanding (receiving), this means that we consider, on the one hand, the biblical record and the Christian tradition and, on the other hand, the life situation of the hearers and the preacher. None of us begins at "zero" when we preach. With regard to the aspect of declaring (giving), it means that, in our sermon, we endeavour to pass on that which has gripped us and which we have understood, in a way that it will most probably affect and inspire the hearers.

Communi-cation as a process The communication process does not, however, end there; the hearers of our sermons are now challenged to pass on and declare what they have received and understood. Thus, we preachers are

---

1   Philosophische Logik, Vol. 1: Von der Wahrheit, Munich 1958, p. 378.

part of the continuing process of understanding and declaring the biblical message. In the ideal case, this leads to the development of a communication and action spirit among the congregation in which the hearers and the preacher allow the biblical message to affect and touch them afresh.

2. COMMUNICATION + GOSPEL = COMMUNICATION OF THE GOSPEL?

If we speak of "communication of the gospel", the above equation seems to suggest itself. We simply assume that "the gospel" is a clearly defined quantity that must now be conveyed to others. Thus, we reduce communication to the question "How do I say it ...?" However, the phrase "communication of the gospel" may be interpreted grammatically in two different directions, which lead to two quite different theological conclusions.

On the one hand, it may mean, as the equation suggests, the declaration of the gospel as a specific content or object (in grammatical terms: *genitivus obiectivus*). On the other hand, however, the gospel may be seen itself as the subject of the communication process (*genitivus subjectivus*). This would mean: the gospel clears the way for itself, it produces, of itself, fellowship and understanding among the people it affects and grips with its truth. These two aspects must be distinguished and, at the same time, seen in relation to one another. The first aspect points to the preacher's skill, to something that can be learnt and checked, which also plays a part in the proclamation of the gospel. After all, hearers and preachers can tell whether a sermon is "good" or "not so good". The second aspect, meanwhile, points to the general fact that the manifest presence of God is not at the preacher's disposal, and that we can, at the very most, merely prepare and create the environment for it in the service. This may also mean that God can override a "poor sermon" or a "lukewarm service" and manifest his presence to bless the congregation. The expression "communication of the gospel" explains to us theologically that, while God has given man the commission to preach (Is. 6:8; Matt. 28:18-20), God himself always remains Lord

The gospel as subject content and as the "power of God"

God entrusts humans with preaching

163

of his grace and of his story with this world (1 Sam. 2:6f; 1 Cor. 12:11). This means: believers are urged, with respect to the communication of the gospel, to gain interest on the talents entrusted to them (cf. Matt. 25:14-30) and yet, at the same time, reminded of the impossible possibility (Karl Barth) of their working and letting God work (cf. Phil. 2:12,13).

It was Ernst Lange who, in the mid-sixties of the 20th century introduced the term communication of the gospel into the church debate about preaching and church building. His description opens up a wide new horizon: "We speak of communication of the gospel instead of 'proclamation' or even 'sermon', because this term both emphasises the dialogue aspect of the process in question and shows that all the functions of the church, which is concerned with interpreting the biblical testimony (from the sermon through to counselling sessions and confirmation classes) are actually phases and aspects of one single process."[2] To Lange, it is important that we "take seriously that which is variable in the human situation before God and in the world, its historicity, its variability, its temporariness."[3] He believes that the purpose of the sermon is "talk to the hearer about his life."[4] Lange sees the sermon as an effort to confer with the hearer, based on the promise of Christ: "For it is in human communication that the promise is made manifest. The community of believers received this building plan already from Jesus. God reveals himself, makes himself known, asserts himself, by bringing human beings into the 'venture of faith' with one another."[5]

Preaching is conferring with the hearers

Thus, preaching may be understood as part of the overall process of God moving towards the world and mankind. To bring people into the venture of faith - what a delightful, worthwhile task! To this day, Lange's emphasis on the multi-dimensional

---

2   E. Lange, Kirche für die Welt. ed. by R. Scholz, München/Gelnhausen 1981, p. 101.
3   Ibid., p. 102.
4   E. Lange in: Die verbesserliche Welt, Stuttgart/Berlin 1968, p. 58.
5   E. Lange, Chancen des Alltags. Überlegungen zur Funktion des christlichen Gottesdienstes in der Gegenwart, Stuttgart/Gelnhausen 1965, p. 110.

164

nature of the comprehensive task of Christians to communicate, and his insistence on the principle of a dialogue involving the preacher and the hearer - or society as a whole - still serve as impulses for practical preaching and church life with a focus on both the bible and everyday experience. The thought-provoking words of the preacher and homiletics teacher Hans Joachim Iwand, however, are no less timeless in showing us the limitations of our human efforts:

> "Sometimes we are reminded of Martin Luther's analogy of the 'cloudburst', that is quickly lapped up by the sun; the going-out of the word of God is and will always remain a contingent event, something that is out of our hands, something that we cannot guarantee or force even with the best theology. God can be silent, too. At any rate, it is important that we are aware of our deficiency. All public relations efforts, all church representation, all endeavours to teach the youth, and the like will remain empty and ineffective if the source from which the church derives its life runs dry. This source is and will always be the 'living word'."[6]

"What is the gospel?" What is this "Living Word", the gospel, about which so much has been said? In the New Testament, especially in the Pauline epistles, the Greek word *euangelion* is used in half the instances without being further defined; in Rom. 2:16, for example, Paul speaks of "his gospel" as he summarises his interpretation of the events concerning Christ. Evidently, the readers then knew what was meant by *evangelion* and therefore did not require an explanation. Nowadays, this is not the case. How many people - inside as well as outside the churches! - still know what the gospel in the biblical sense is? In the following, we will give a basic outline of the meaning of gospel:[7]

---

6   Predigtmeditationen I, 4th Ed., Göttingen 1984, p. 528.
7   Cf. W. Klaiber, Call and Response. Biblical Foundations of a Theology of Evangelism, Nashville 1997, pp. 29-162.

The message that brings joy   The gospel is the good news (Is. 52:7), which - according to the biblical testimony - is proclaimed against the background of the advancing righteousness (Ps. 98:2) and reign of God (Rev. 21:3f). The biblical gospel is God speaking and revealing himself in his creation, in the history of his chosen people and, finally, in the work and destiny of Jesus Christ, the final fulfilment of which is still to come (Phil. 2:10ff). Not only did Jesus proclaim the gospel; he fulfilled it himself, single-mindedly and with all the consequences: by the love he showed towards all people, by his miracles as the visible sign of God's dominion over all the destructive powers, and finally by the cross and the resurrection.

Fruitful life   The intent of the gospel, which is upheld essentially by the love of God towards the human race (Gen. 2:21ff; Tit. 3:4), is a complete, fruitful life (Hebrew: *shalom*) that has been promised precisely to those who cannot attain it by their own strength (Is. 61:1ff; Matt. 5:3ff). Thus, the gospel is a word against all appearances, because the message proceeds from the Spirit of God, it carries in itself renewing and creating power. Nowhere is **Justification** this more evident than in the justification of the godless (Rom. 3:23f) and the establishment of a new relationship with God (Jer. 31:31f; Rom. 5:1f). Thus, the gospel is always a call to turn around and believe (Mi. 7:18; Mk. 1:15) and - in New Testament terms - a call to wholeheartedly follow Jesus Christ together with other believers (Matt. 28:18-20). What the bible calls salvation is, after all, never an individual possession; it is only realised through fellowship with other Christians and through responsibly serving God in the world. The intent of the gospel is to change and shape **Change** lives (Phil. 2:12f); through the Spirit of God, its message liberates (Gal. 5:1) and points the way (Is. 58:7; Gal. 2:20).

In the context of this chapter, the following three aspects of the good news of the bible are of particular importance to us:

The answer   (1) Anyone who wants to become a communicator of the gospel can only really do so if they are convinced that the good news recorded in the bible still remains the answer today to the questions of man about the beginning and the end, salvation and

166

life, righteousness and justice, and hope for the future. Someone who has not experienced the gospel as the good news and a life-giving hope will hardly be able to pass it on in a convincing way.

(2) The gospel remains both an invitation and an obligation for those who have heard and received it to entrust every area of their lives more and more to its message (this is what is the biblical term sanctification means). **Invitation and obligation**

(3) Finally, it remains the commission to stand up for the gospel in word and deed, both in private and in public, with the confidence we now have in the power of God's message, in a manner that is inviting and appropriate for our time. We agree in this point with Hans-Joachim Iwands, who believes: **Commission**

> "Then we will soon come to realise that 'modern man' is not, after all, as incapable of receiving as we think, that he is in actual fact looking for steadiness and steadfastness, that he does not want us to chase after him all the time; he is already chased around and is therefore looking for a hand that will lead and guide him ..."[8]

II. Some findings of communication research

In the following, we will introduce two of the countless models of communication theory published throughout the 20th century and examine to what extent they can be applied to our subject.

1. A BASIC MODEL: COMMUNICATION AS TRANSMISSION OF INFORMATION

The basic cybernetic model is probably the most well-known and most easily understandable model of communication.[9] It involves three factors: the sender - the channel/message - the receiver, which combine in a controlled (Greek: *kybernetes*, helmsman) process by which information is transmitted.

---

8   H.-J. Iwand, loc. cit., p. 503f.
9   Cf. F. v. Cube, Was ist Kybernetik, Bremen 1967.

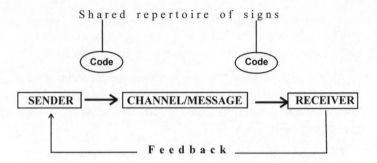

The sender-receiver model focuses in particular on the exchange of information: the sender encodes their information by putting it in words, gestures or movements and hopes, after they have sent the encoded information, that the reception apparatus of their opposite will pick these codes up and decode them correctly, so that the intended message can finally reach the receiver's consciousness. Two things become clear here: Firstly, in order for the exchange of information to be successful, the sender and receiver must have a common social and linguistic framework or a "shared repertoire of signs". Secondly, this model points to potential sources of errors in the communication process: besides the message, there may be "noises" in the channel, disruptions (background noise, distractions, emotional inconsistencies) that may distort the information and hamper the communication flow. Positive factors (shared experiences, non-verbal signals), on the other hand, can facilitate the exchange of information. Moreover, feedback from the receiver to the sender can show whether the intended information arrived or not.

This basic model was adapted by Karl-Wilhelm Dahm to describe the preaching process.[10]

---

10 K.-W. Dahm, Hören und Verstehen. Kommunikationssozi ologische Überlegungen zur gegenwärtigen Predigtnot. In: Predigtstudien IV/2. Reprinted in: A. Beutel/V. Drehsen/H. M. Müller (Ed.) Homiletisches Lesebuch, 2nd. Ed., Tübingen 1989, p. 242-252.

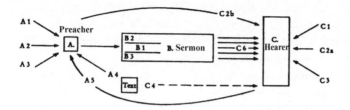

Source: Karl-Wilhelm Dahm, Hören und Verstehen, in: Homiletisches Lesebuch, p. 246. and elsewhere.

On the basis of the cybernetic communication model, Dahm illustrates the "system of the sermon" involving the following three factors:

- A: Sender = Preacher
- B: Channel/Message = Sermon
- C: Receiver = Hearers

The decisive thing about Dahm's model is the fact that he assigns what he calls "background variables" to each of the three factors. By this he means additional influences which serve to further illustrate the variable nature of the communication process "sermon". **"Background variables"**

(A: 1-5): The preacher is not an invariable factor, but a human being who is exposed to many influences. Dahm suggests the following influences on preachers:
1. various features of their personality
2. the way they see their role
3. specific events of the day
4. the biblical text
5. their expectations regarding the reaction of the congregation (feedback).

(B: 1-3): The sermon is not merely one single message, but a "package" of messages which is determined by various individual factors, of which Dahm lists the following:
1. the subject
2. the rhetorical presentation, and
3. the general atmosphere of the service

(C: 1-6): The hearers include many different people, each of whom is at the interface of various influencing forces. In this context, Dahm mentions the following "background variables":

1. various personalities and biographies
2. specific ideas and expectations regarding the service, the sermon and the preacher
3. events of the day
4. the text (which, according to Dahm, is usually not remembered!)
5. feedback (which often does not take place!) and, finally,
6. the "package" of the sermon.

The advantage of the cybernetic communication model is its focus on the exchange of information. However, communication is more than that. This is true particularly of the sermon and the proclamation of the gospel in general. Dahm's contribution to homiletic research lies in the fact that he showed the complexity of the "system of the sermon" by applying concepts from the field of communication studies to the preaching process. His analysis of the sermon as "one-way communication" was sobering and illuminating at the same time, as it aptly described the state of competition in which the preaching process finds itself as it is affected by the various influencing factors listed above. (This list may easily be extended!) At the time, the author calls for a group discussion to complement the sermon. This is successfully practised in many churches today. However, in the context of communicating the gospel further, this can - like the sermon - only be yet *one* more building block.

The sermon is a reciprocal process between the preacher and the hearers In recent times, the sermon has increasingly been seen again as a reciprocal process, taking place between the preacher and the hearers, despite the fact that it is usually delivered in the form of a monologue. The sermon is so to speak an extract from the broader dialogue between the preacher and the congregation. The preacher must not be restricted to the active role of the sender, nor the hearer to the passive role of the receiver, i.e. that of the object. With respect to preaching, we must therefore take into account the fact that the preacher and the hearer both refer to the text (or the topic), which may not receive enough attention if we apply the model too rigidly. As the preacher and the hearers, we both stand before God, whose assurances and demands regarding our lives should become effective as we together listen to the words of the bible.

2. AN EXTENDED MODEL: HUMAN COMMUNICATION AS A FOURFOLD EVENT

Among the most influential publications in recent times in the area of communication psychology of the German tongue are those of the Hamburg psychologist Friedemann Schulz von Thun. In particular, his three volumes entitled "Miteinander reden" (Talking to each other) should be mentioned.[11] The author examines communication in a whole range of everyday situations (Vol. 1) by means of the so-called "message square". He then develops eight "communication styles", by combining various psychological approaches (Vol. 2). Finally, he shows ways to a form of communication that is appropriate to the specific person and situation (Vol. 3).

The Hamburg communication model

a) The "message square"

A statement/message that we receive or send actually contains several messages which have various effects. We have all experienced misunderstandings resulting from this fact. The theory of the "message square" can help to clarify and resolve issues in many contexts - including the context of the sermon, as will be shown later.

This theory is based on the distinction between a subject and a relationship aspect in human communication made by Paul Watzlawick et al.[12] Their central thesis is as follows: "All communication has a subject and a relationship aspect, with the latter determining the former." Schulz von Thun takes this

Sub-aspects of communication

---

11 F. Schulz von Thun, Miteinander reden 1-3, 3 Vols., Reinbe k 1981, 1989, 1998.
12 P. Watzlawick/J. H. Beavin/D. D. Jackson, Pragmatics of Human Communication. A Study of Interactional Patterns, New York 1967.

concept further: he divides the relationship aspect further into three, thus arriving at the "message square".

Let us take a closer look at an everyday scene from the perspective of communication psychology:

Source: Friedemann Schulz von Thun, Miteinander reden 1, 1981, pp. 25 and 31

Content aspect   The *content aspect* refers to the content of the message or statement: What factual information is conveyed? In the above example, we are told something about the state of the traffic light: it is on green. The content aspect is always at the centre of the message when it is about the "subject matter". However, precisely where this is stressed, there is often more to the statement!

The *self-disclosure aspect* shows that, whenever we make a statement, we are also giving a "taste" of our own selves. Even

when we are not speaking about ourselves something of our **Self-**
personality and our present emotional state shines through. In **disclosure**
every conversation, we learn, something about the person of the **aspect**
sender, be it directly through what is said or indirectly through
other circumstances such as body language, tone of voice, gestures
and facial expressions. In our example, the self-disclosure is: I am
an attentive passenger and, besides - I'm in a hurry!

There are two basic variants regarding the self-disclosure
aspect of a conversation: we can either use our messages for the
purpose of presentation ourselves (the offensive variant: showing
oneself at one's best, impressing) or for the purpose of hiding
ourselves (the defensive variant: not "letting the cat out of the
bag", deliberately belittling ourselves). In addition to these two
variants, there is also the possibility of accidental self-disclosure
(revealing one's weaknesses), which can create embarrassing
situations. With the self-disclosure aspect we have touched on the
area of genuineness; authenticity is an essential criterion for
success in human communication.

The *relationship aspect* of a message reveals something about
what we think of the opposite and how we perceive the **Relationship**
relationship we have with our opposite. It is a matter of, "it's not **aspect**
what you say, but the way that you say it". This aspect is
determined initially by the perspective of the sender, who reveals
in his/her statement what kind of relationship exists between the
two parties involved in the communicative event. The receiver
may consequently feel accepted and treated as an equal, or
belittled and patronised. Let us return to our example. "It's
green!" means, in real terms: the sender is telling the receiver that
he regards her as either not capable or not willing to drive in the
best possible way. The relationship aspect of communication is
probably the most common source of errors in the interaction
between people. The example makes this clear: the woman (who
will agree with the passenger with regard to the content of the
statement!) responds at the relationship level by asking: "Who's
driving, you or me?"

It is here, within the relationship aspect, that the distinction between verbal and non-verbal communication is most relevant. While information is transmitted in verbal communication through linguistic signs, non-verbal communication occurs through stimuli, which reach our consciousness through various perception channels (the human senses). Sources of non-verbal signals include: body language, pictures, noises, scents, physical contact, changes of temperature, etc. Whether we are aware of it or not, these factors significantly affect the atmosphere of the conversation and, consequently, the communication between people.

Appeal aspect
Finally, the *appeal aspect* focuses on the question: what do we, as senders want to cause the receiver to do? A "message" is not just empty words without any purpose; it has a specific "intent" or function. We want the receiver to respond to what we say by doing or refraining from doing something, or by feeling or thinking something.[13] In our example, the appeal is unambiguous: Come on, drive!

In our everyday lives, we experience that words can comfort and encourage, but also hurt and destroy. This close connection between speaking and acting was described by John L. Austin and John R. Searle in their speech act theory.[14] A person who speaks acts and wants to influence his/her opposite by what s/he says. This is true especially in the case of an appeal. Now, it is necessary to distinguish between overt appeals (e.g. clear instructions or verbalised expectations), which are can be easily recognised as appeals, and covert appeals (e.g. demanding admiration or compassion), a kind of "hidden agenda" in the conversation which is a form of exercising power and may have lasting effects. Finally, there are paradox appeals, where obeying

---

13 Already in the 1940s, H. D. Lasswell already showed by his formula "Who says what in what form with what intention?" how human communication is effect-related.

14 J. L. Austin, Speech act theory, York University (1975), and J. R. Searle, Speech Acts: An Essay in the Philosophy of Language, Strawson, PF (1964/1969)

the command in actual fact means not obeying it (e.g. "Be spontaneous!" or "Do it willingly!"). It is only in the case of overt appeals that the communication takes place on the basis of mutual respect between the sender and the hearer. Overt appeals take the strain out of the relationship between the two parties involved in the conversation and enable them to respond with a clear *yes* or *no*. If, however, the other three aspects of the message are clearly subjected to the appeal and we have to assume, at the same time, that the opposite does not (immediately) realise this, this must be regarded as manipulation.

b) The "four-eared receiver"

Thus far, we have looked at the message square primarily from the sender's perspective. We saw that a message contains a whole bundle of sub-messages, which are sent simultaneously via four different channels. Consequently, there has to be a corresponding "four-eared receiver" at the other end, who receives these sub-

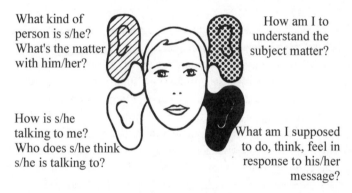

What kind of person is s/he? What's the matter with him/her?

How am I to understand the subject matter?

How is s/he talking to me? Who does s/he think s/he is talking to?

What am I supposed to do, think, feel in response to his/her message?

messages, and decodes and evaluates them.

Source: Friedemann Schulz von Thun, Miteinander reden 1, 1981, p.45.

Schulz von Thun stresses that the receiver of our message can **Free choice** basically choose freely which ear they want to open or close! The fact that the other person can do with my message so to speak

175

"whatever they like" again suggests that there is great potential for misunderstandings. Moreover, true communication is often made difficult by one-sided hearing habits (a particular responsiveness **Hearing** to certain subjects, particular roles assigned to the hearer by **habits** him/herself or by others, the psychological condition of the hearer). Some people have a specially developed "content ear" and will therefore process anything that is said at the factual subject level. Others have a very sensitive "self-disclosure ear" and will therefore interpret a question such as "Can you see that aeroplane up there?" as an expression of their opposites emotional condition. People with a strongly developed "relationship ear" will have a tendency to assess the interpersonal "chemistry" all the time and to take things personally. Finally, people with an oversized "appeal ear" will always be obliging and therefore have a tendency to be driven by the expectations of others than by their own initiative.

The time dimension
c) The communicative event as interplay between the sender and the receiver

All that has been said thus far regarding the "processing of data" by the sender and hearer merely reflects what happens at a particular moment in the communicative event. In real life, however, there is a further dimension: time. In a dialogue, the roles of the sender and hearer are constantly being exchanged. As well as the progression of the conversation at the subject level, there is also a constant comparison at the other three levels between that which was said and that which has recognisably reached the opposite. That which is sent by the respective sender as a "statement" may coincide with the underlying inner disposition ("inner statement")[15] or deviate from it. Every statement **The sender** is aimed at the "inner statements" of the receiver, and the sender expects a perceivable response from the respective receiver (again in the form of a statement). The following comprehensive model of the communication process illustrates this.

---

15 By "inner statements" F. Schulz von Thun means the combination of thoughts, feelings, presuppositions, and intentions that form the basis of a statement.

Source: Friedemann Schulz von Thun, Miteinander reden 1, 1981, p.45.

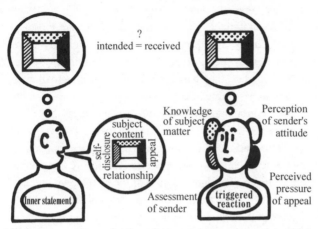

All human communication has an inner dynamic which is determined by a sequence of actions and events that structure progression of the exchange like punctuation marks (greetings, gestures, rituals). This means that, in everyday communication, there is usually no clear beginning or end of a verbal exchange; rather, there are always previous experiences (with resulting preconceptions and fears) which enter into the process as "inner statements". Moreover, there are additional risks and sources of conflict that result from acquired, recurring patterns of behaviour and reactions and may prevent the parties from understanding one another.[16] Even if the **Inner** parties choose an appropriate beginning or conclusion for their conversation, they nonetheless have to relate somehow to one another **dynamic** before and afterwards. The communicative event may therefore be compared to a cycle. If we include what has just been said, the illustration will be that of a spiral which is open at either end. This illustration accounts for the fact that, in interpersonal communication, we may go backwards as well as forwards.

---

16 In transaction analysis (TA), the term "playing" is used to describe this . Cf. E. Berne, Games People Play, New York 1964.

3. COMMUNICATION OF THE GOSPEL IN THE LIGHT OF THE HAMBURG MODEL

Like all mental tools designed to clarify and improve communication between people, this psychological approach may serve as an aid. The preaching of the gospel has a spiritual dimension which can never be fully described by worldly methods. On the other hand, however, it is undeniable that the sermon and other forms of Christian testimony are always founded on a basic communicative structure. Alone for that reason, it would be useful to make a connection between this approach and the "communication of the gospel" (in the wider as well as the narrow sense of the phrase). Before turning to preaching as a specific instance of communication of the gospel, we will consider the overall task of communicating the gospel from a theological perspective in the light of the above model.

Let us begin with an exercise:

🖎 **Exercise** Look at the following cartoon and then try to describe what is happening with the help of Schulz von Thun's communication model.

Quelle: AMD der Westfälischen Landeskirche, Dortmund

178

The statements of the senders may be said to have the following **inner statements:**

- Content aspect: "Everyone needs Christ, including you!" (John 3:16; Acts 4:12)
- Self-disclosure aspect: "The gospel of Jesus Christ is so important to us that we are even willing to go from door to door to share it with complete strangers!"
- Relationship aspect: "We have what you need!"[17]
- Appeal aspect: "Invite us in, listen to what we have to say - be converted!"

On the receiver side, we may identify the following implied statements, which point to the corresponding "inner statements": **The receiver**

- Content aspect: "I haven't got a clue what you're talking about."
- Self-disclosure aspect: "Do I look like I'm lost? Don't waste my time! Your religious gibberish doesn't make sense, anyway!"
- Relationship aspect: "Let's not bother! We're not really interested in each other, anyway!"
- Appeal aspect: "Your appeal is going nowhere. And anyway: You should reconsider your choice of words!"

The basic distinction between content and relationship aspects has shown us in relation to the task of communicating the gospel that, while we must distinguish between our testimony through words and our testimony through deeds, they are nonetheless related. If, in applying this theory, we ignore the theological truth that God can even speak through Balaam's donkey (Num. 22:28ff.), we can hardly expect the gospel to be received by the people around us as the good news, unless it is accompanied by credible assurances within the other three aspects. Yet we are not taking away from the sovereignty of God's workings if we suggest that the human circumstances and the individuals involved play a

---

17 This is a case of complementary communication of giving and receiving/knowing and not knowing, without the participants seeking to establish any real contact.

Christ's ambassadors significant part in the communication of the gospel.[18] Christians are "Christ's ambassadors" (2 Cor. 5:20) who have the "treasure" of the gospel in "jars of clay" (2 Cor. 4:7) and can therefore only pass it on that way. In recent times, the "body language of the body of Christ"[19] has therefore been stressed as being essential to a credible testimony of Christ in our day. The apostle Paul mentions the key word in this context, love, in his letter to the Thessalonian Christians (1 Thess. 2:8): "We loved you so much that we were delighted to share with you not only the gospel of God but our lives as well ..."

In relation to the content aspect of sharing the gospel, the Christian church has to ask itself the question: Are we sufficiently clear about what we want to communicate, what "the gospel" means? Every generation will have to determine that for itself. Let us look at what Ernst Lange has to say in this regard: "The homiletic act is an endeavour to communicate. The object of this endeavour is the Christian tradition as it is relevant to the present situation of the hearer and the congregation as a whole. The assurance of this communication of the gospel is the agreement and the consent of faith regarding the profession of the Christian church that Jesus Christ is Lord, more specifically, that he is *my* Lord in every situation of my life."[20]

Self-disclosure and relationship aspect With respect to the aspect of self-disclosure and relationship, we can say: Unless we reduce the communication of the gospel to conveying a message in a factually correct way, we assume that God is interested in the whole person. Be it in a sermon or in religious education, in Christian social work or in a personal conversation about the Christian faith: the people with whom we work and interact want - like we ourselves - to be perceived and taken seriously as a true partner in a conversation, i.e. with all

---

18 A survey conducted in the German-speaking countries of Europe showed that 76% of the 1.600 people questioned came to the Christian faith and the church through personal relationships, i.e. friends/family, cf. C. A. Schwarz, Grundkurs Evangelisation, Emmelsbüll 1993, p. 17.

19 W. Abraham, The Logic of Evangelism, Grand Rapids/Michigan 1989, p. 13.

20 E. Range, Predigen als Beruf, 2nd Ed. Munich 1987, p. 20.

their personal, job-related, physical, and psychological needs (relationship aspect). They will be more likely to receive the message from someone who behaves as a true partner (self-disclosure aspect) than from someone who acts like the two men in the cartoon. The gospel of Jesus Christ is more a person-message than a subject-message. This is why we as believers, as paid or voluntary workers of the church, must act as people just as **Subject** we expect our opposite to act as a person.[21] The Latin word **aspect** *communicate* contains the root *communio* (community). Therefore the goal of the *communicatio* of the gospel of God has been successful if the sender and the receiver are both part of the community of the people of God and interact through the same person-message.

Finally, the appeal aspect: Nowadays, people will rather be willing to respond positively to an appeal if they are themselves convinced of the subject matter concerned, and if they have **Appeal** developed trust in the people who represent this matter. Where **aspect** such a relationship of trust exists, we can speak without restraint and therefore boldly present the appeal-aspect of the biblical message[22] as well - without being perceived as a know-it-all. When appealing to our opposite, it is important to find the balance between the required urgency on the one hand, and the freedom of the hearer on the other hand, which we may not infringe upon if we do not want to be guilty of manipulating.

The following fable by the Danish philosopher and Theologian Sören Kierkegaard shows that the greatest challenge to successful communication of the gospel is for the believers to trust continually in the reality and power of God's workings, indeed to depend on them.

---

21 The Latin word *per-sonare* (to sound through, for example through a face mask in an antique theatre play) expresses a similar concept to the described above as "inner statement" and "(outer) statement".

22 It is in the assurance of God's love ("gospel") that his claim to our lives ("law") has its root: this is evident in the call to repentance and to a life in holiness (for both the individual and society as a whole).

"Christians live like geese on a farm. Every seven days, a parade is held and the eloquent gander stands on the fence and gabbles about the miracle of the geese; he tells them about the deeds of their ancestors, who once dared to fly, and about the mercy of the creator, who gave the geese wings and the instinct to fly. The geese are deeply moved, they bow their heads in awe, they praise the sermon and the eloquent gander. But that is it. One thing they never do - fly. Instead they go to lunch. They don't fly, for the grain is good and the farm yard is safe ..."[23]

4. THE WORK OF THE PREACHER IN THE LIGHT OF THE HAMBURG COMMUNICATION MODEL

(1) In the training and development of (future) preachers, we have found it helpful, when transferring and applying the findings of the above communication model, to begin by having the students analyse their own preaching with regard to the four aspects of the message square. For this purpose, we suggest, the **Directed** use of a colour code, whereby we assign different colours to a **questions** number of key questions that correspond with the four aspects of communication.

> ➤ BLUE: What is the information content of my sermon? What is the gospel, what is the "law" that calls man into question, which I have been commissioned to preach?
>
> ➤ YELLOW: Where does the congregation learn something about me as a person, my faith, my questions, my hopes, my fears?
>
> ➤ RED: What does my sermon reveal about the way I view the church and the relationship between myself, as the preacher, and the congregation?
>
> ➤ GREEN: Where do I appeal (overtly or covertly) to the minds, the emotions, the will, and the behaviour of the hearers?
>
> Finally: How are the four aspects weighted and how can this weighting be theologically justified (in the light of the relevant biblical text)?

---

23 Cited in W. Hoffsümmer, Kurzgeschichten 3, 4th Ed., Mainz 1990, p. 59.

182

You may want to try this method by examining the manuscript of one of your past sermons or a sermon on which you are ✍ **Exercise** currently working in this manner. If we assume that any message can contain all four aspects, the purpose of this exercise is to determine which aspect is emphasised most in that particular sermon.

- Do all four colours feature in your sermon manuscript?
- Does one particular colour dominate and, if so, why?
- To which sentences could you assign more than one colour?
- What else did you notice?

The proportions of the colours of the sermon message determine to a large extent the complexion of the sermon. It is only when we look at the manuscript as a whole that we can ascertain which is the main statement that actually gives the sermon its character, and which secondary statements are made at the other levels of communication. In doing so, we must pay special attention to the sentences or sections of the sermon that have been marked with more than one colour, as they can often lead to misunderstandings. The exercise with the key questions can serve as a tool to help bring out the intended message of the sermon in the best possible way. This exercise can be especially illuminating if the intended message of the preacher is later compared with the colour-coded impressions of hearers or readers of the sermon manuscript in a discussion.

Generally speaking, it is about ensuring that the prepared sermon is appropriate to the text or topic, the person of the preacher, and the hearers, in other words, within the framework of what we introduced in chapter 1 as the homiletic triangle.

(2) Next, we will consider the communicative aspects of preaching, again with the help of the message square.[24]

According to Schulz von Thun, the success or failure of a conversation is dependent on a number of factors, which we

---

24 In the following, we will refer to: F. Schulz von Thun, Miteinander reden 1, loc. cit. p. 116f., 129f., 158f., and G. Theißen, The Sign Language of Faith, London 1995.

Clearly expressing the main aspect believe can also be applied to the communication of the gospel through preaching. In both instances, the communication aim is to achieve clarity with reference to the message square. It is always advisable to express the main aspect of what one intends to say clearly and directly. This sounds plausible when referring to factual information or self-disclosure statements. In practice, however, many misunderstandings result from the fact that relationship and appeal aspects are often only contained as overtones and undertones in seemingly pure factual statements. For this reason, we need to pay special attention to these latter aspects and have the courage to express them clearly.

Content must be factual and comprehensible At the content level, we must make sure that we argue in a factual and comprehensible way. At the self-disclosure level, we must be genuine and relevant to the situation. Unless there is a general attitude of acceptance based on mutual respect at the relationship level, there is little chance of a factual discussion or appeal being successful. An appeal is most likely to achieve its goal if the receiver can see that the sender has first received it for themselves, thus showing that they are willing to accept responsibility for what they are saying. These issues will be further discussed below.

a) The content aspect of preaching

Prospects of preaching In other areas of life we give people with expert knowledge the opportunity to present their thoughts coherently and therefore almost always in a relatively long speech. It is impossible to imagine the political culture of a democracy without debate in the form of speeches. Where else other than in a sermon do church members get the opportunity to have a biblical passage or a topic of the Christian faith expounded to them in a clear and structured way. Many preachers underestimate the need for factual, didactic preaching that presents theological information in a rhetorically effective way! Usually hearers will appreciate preaching that is biblically sound and relevant to their everyday lives and the social reality that surrounds them. In this area, the sermons of trained theologians and those of lay preachers may and should differ with

184

regard to their emphasis. Nonetheless, both will seek to ensure that their theological statements are relevant to the hearers as well as factually correct.

In the case of text-based sermons, two things are important: In order for a sermon to be appropriate in respect of its content, we **Content of** must not only consider the theological content of the biblical text, **the text** but also seek to grasp its linguistic character. The preacher must try to get a feel of the text that will help determine in what form it should be delivered. Although there will very often be a clear correspondence between the content and the form of the sermon, this aspect should at least be considered. Thus, a didactic text taken from a Pauline epistle will automatically suggest a didactic form (high proportion of blue), while the interpretation of a Psalm **Form of** will lead the preacher and the congregation (must therefore **the text** include red and yellow!) into prayer. Of course, every sermon will essentially want to lead the hearers towards an encounter with God and encourage them, as in Kierkegaard's fable, to put their trust in the presence and the promise of God!

We have already addressed the key of comprehensibility when we talked about the sermon as a type of speech. Comprehensibility is essential to communicating the subject content and will always be appreciated by the hearers. Friedemann Schulz von Thun lists four "comprehensibility factors" in communication, from which a sermon may benefit as well:

- *Simplicity* (opposite: complexity) in the choice of lexis and syntax: clear language, short sentences, familiar words, **Simplicity** explanation of specialist terminology. By simplicity we do not mean simplistic.

- *Structuredness and coherence* (opposite: confusion, incoher- **Structured-** ence) regarding the organisation and presentation of thoughts **ness and** make it easier for the hearers to follow the sermon. Thus, **coherence** attention may be drawn towards climaxes or key statements in the sermon, which the hearers are then able to take home with them.

Brevity and conciseness

• *Brevity and conciseness* (opposite: long-windedness): The preacher respects the limits of the hearers' ability to remain attentive. They avoid telegraphese at the one end of the spectrum and endless argumentation at the other.

Additional stimulation

• *Additional stimulation* (opposite: no additional stimulation): Language offers an abundance of means by which we can season our sermons. Puns and proverbs, but also the use of pictures, symbols and objects serve as additional stimulants, that increase the motivation and attentiveness of the hearers and, at the same time, reiterate the factual content of the sermon. In this context, Gerd Theißen uses the term "measured divergences". By this he means, for example, "a slight defamiliarisation of everyday language, which allows us to see familiar words in a new light, the use of traditional biblical language in new contexts in an unusual way, playing with familiar jargon in a humorous way ..." These "measured divergences" may also be applied to the sermon structure, and to the use of stories, pictures and objects in the sermon. A well-chosen additional point, an unexpected turn at the end, a carefully selected object to take home after the service, all serve to reiterate the biblical message and help the hearers understand and remember it.

What has been said above shows that comprehensibility, motivation, graphicness and consideration for the limits of the hearers' attentiveness are not concessions that the preacher makes to the hearers, but basic conditions of preaching, the purpose of which is always to be received.

b) The self-disclosure aspect of preaching

It is difficult to say how must self-disclosure is appropriate in a sermon.[25] Self-disclosure in the sermon may be direct ("But I tell you...!") or indirect by way of the preaching style (comforting, demanding, didactic style).

---

25 Cf. the thoughts on the "I" in the pulpit in Chapter 8.

We will begin by looking at direct self-disclosure. Preachers should neither act like a non-person nor focus unduly on themself. However, the hearers should get the feeling that they are looking at a real flesh-and-blood human being who is able to talk freely about self in the sermon. They should also feel that the preacher is someone who is trying to lead a spiritual life. This may also require discretion when it comes to expressing one's own views in public. For this purpose, preachers can make use of the linguistic options of self-concealment as well as self-presentation. Such options include we-statements, it-statements and one-statements, and "veiling techniques ... aimed hiding and camouflaging those aspects of the preacher's personality that he perceives as negative."[26] Behind many you-messages there may well, in reality, be an (avoided) I-message.

As with the subject aspect, clarity and unambiguity will pay off in the area of self-disclosure, particularly in respect of the (long-term) relationship between hearers and preachers. If preachers **Courage to** have the courage to disclose themselves to the hearers, they will **disclose self** be clear about where they are with them. Preachers revealing themselves increases the potential for conflict; in the long run, however, such a person will have a better chance of leading the congregation deeper into the subject matter than a person who avoids taking a clear stand, because of wanting to please everyone.

Next, we will look at indirect self-disclosure. All preachers have their own style of preaching, which is good. The preaching style is inextricably connected with the personality of the preacher and their respective biography. Friedemann Schulz von Thun distinguishes eight "communication styles", which may be applied to preaching as well.[27]

---

26 F. Schulz von Thun, Miteinander reden 1, loc. cit., p. 108
27 F. Schulz von Thun, Miteinander reden 2, loc. cit., pp. 61-241.

| The needy dependent style | The helping style | The selfless style | The aggressive degrading style |

| The façade style | The dominant controlling style | The distant style | The sharing dramatising style |

Being aware of one's own style is helpful; critically developing it further is a worthwhile endeavour. A person who has to preach regularly will try to widen their scope so as to avoid remaining in their own comfort zone. At the same time, however, we must be aware of the fact that we cannot completely change our personality if we are to remain truthful and genuine.

Genuine-ness of the preacher Finally, the preacher must be genuine in a very general sense, namely in the sense of credibility (integrity). Does what the preacher says reflect their lifestyle? Paul wrote to the Corinthians: "You are a letter from Christ ... known and read by everybody" (2 Cor. 3:2,3), thus reminding us of the importance of a living testimony for the communication of the gospel. On the other hand, however: "We live by faith, not by sight" (2 Cor. 5,7).

Promise-orientated preaching If we only preach the things that we have already put into practice in our lives, we are not going far enough. God's promises are meant for a "correctable world" (Ernst Lange)!

The truthfulness (authenticity) of the preacher helps to build a bridge of understanding between the message and the addressees, because the preacher is conscious of their commitment and obligation to both. A sermon is appealing and credible if the preacher strives towards a "controlled subjectivity" (Wilfried Engemann) with respect to their disclosure of self. Thus, both the experience of vulnerability and success can have a place in the sermon.

c) The relationship aspect of preaching

Just like in everyday life, we must pay special attention to the relationship aspects in preaching, as it is here that we find many opportunities, but also many a stumbling block for the preaching of the gospel. The sermon has the character of an address. It therefore presupposes a relationship between the preacher and the congregation, which then becomes audible and perceptible in the preaching process. Some preachers address their hearers in a **Type of** more formal way; others prefer a less formal address. The **address** personality of the preacher and the specific situation determine which type of address is more appropriate in a given context. In both cases, the central question regarding the relationship aspect is: What comes across as being our image of the hearers and our perception of the church?

Examine your sample sermon once more with regard to the two questions: which you-messages ("This is what I think about you") **Exercise** and which we-messages ("This is what I think of how we relate to each other") have you discovered? Does this reflect what you intend to say?

Sermon hearers want to know that they are understood, taken **Addressing** seriously, respected and accepted. A patronising and belittling **the** attitude is not consistent with the spirit of a Protestant sermon, **congregation** which always wants to help the hearers to "walk with their heads **as** held high" (Helmut Gollwitzer). It is therefore important that we **responsible** address the hearers in a winsome manner as responsible partners, **equals** whose freedom we recognise and respect. Werner Jetter put it like this: "The preacher must treat his hearer as a mature person and learn to hear his own words through the hearer's ears."[28]

---

28   W. Jetter, Wem predigen wir?, Stuttgart 1964, p. 46.

Don't curry favour

The relationship level is not about arousing the hearers' sympathy or appealing to them at all costs. Critical hearers will easily recognise any attempt to curry favour (i.e. the use of relationship messages for the wrong purpose) and respond to it with apathy or aggression. A sermon is most likely to meet with open ears and hearts if the preacher succeeds in creating an atmosphere of mutual appreciation in which both sides can learn together (before God). In order to achieve this, the preacher should try to draw closer to the hearers in the sermon; by this we do not, however, mean that one should to intrude on their privacy or even to "sit on their laps". Closeness and care are particularly important when we have to criticise something about the congregation on the basis of the gospel. Yet this can only be successful if there is a certain degree of distance between preacher and congregation and, at the same time, tact and a basic attitude of acceptance is displayed. Thus, closeness and distance are two opposite ends of the spectrum, and the preacher must find the appropriate balance somewhere in between these two extremes. Karl Barth identified the pivot of this balancing act (with reference to 1 Cor. 13): love, in which closeness and distance are adequately expressed.

Love

"The preacher must love his church. He must not want to be without his church and must know: I belong to these people and want to share with them what I have received from God. Speaking in tongues of men and of angels will profit nothing, if there is no love".[29]

The limits of aiming at a target audience

After all, it will never be possible to fully assess and adequately address the hearers' situation. The individual situations in life and the views of God and the world represented within the congregation are too varied. As preachers, we very often have to depend on general observations and statements; many issues can only be assumed. Preachers who know their congregation well, for example through conversations or home visits, can be more specific. The sermon can share the joys and

---

29   K. Barth, Homiletik, 2nd Ed., Zurich (1966) 198 5, p. 67.

190

sorrows of the church, however, always bearing in mind that it must respect the privacy of individual members.

Finally, we will look at an example to illustrate how one can build a relationship with the hearers through general statements based on shrewd observation in everyday situations. If the hearers get the feeling, "The preacher understands us!" and develop a kind of "inner agreement" with them they will also receive the factual and appellative messages prescribed by the text on which the present example is based (Matt. 7: 24-27, conclusion of the sermon on the mount).

On a rainy Sunday during the wet summer of the year 2000, Rev. Hans-Martin Niethammer speaks to the hearts of the hearers as he begins his sermon with the following words:

"These days, everyone seems to be talking about the weather. What about us? Are we also concerned with the weather? Why shouldn't we be? After all, it plays such an important part even in this parable of Jesus. The weather is always a topic, the topic, when people meet. I therefore refuse to believe that this is just due to embarrassment or a lack of other topics. Could it be that there is more to it? Why is the weather report one of the most popular programmes on television? Of course, the weather affects us, a lot of things depend on it.

Last week we were waiting anxiously, wondering whether the boys brigade outing would have to be cancelled. In the end it was "washed out". Let's hope the weather will be better during the holidays, or it will be dreary. Many of our plans depend on the weather, but also the way we feel is affected by the weather. Some people are extremely sensitive to the weather; the way they feel in their bodies is closely connected with the weather. And even more so our moods. When the sun is shining we all immediately feel better. We are all in some way dependent on the weather.

We don't really realise how much we depend on the weather until it causes a disaster. When a low pressure sweeps across our land, when torrential rains threaten our crops or floods cover an entire region we feel frightened and helpless. Especially, as we have reason to fear nowadays that these phenomena may occur more frequently. Are they perhaps initial signs of a coming climatic disaster? We already ask ourselves this question every time the winter turns out milder or the summer wetter than usual.

I believe there is no other topic that shows us so clearly how dependent we are. In the midst of a world in which nothing seems impossible for us, it is the weather that makes us realise the limitations of our possibilities and predictions.

When we talk about the weather we are therefore talking about life. We speak of the storms that sweep over us, but also of the 'sun shine of our lives' and 'a place in the sun'. Sometimes we are 'left out in the cold' by someone or a trouble comes over us like a flood. Life seems changeable and unpredictable like the weather- and therefore always at risk. Exposed to all the assaults of our climate.

Fortunately, however, we are not left completely unprotected. After all, we are clever. We would be foolish if all we did was complain about the weather! We can do something. And we must do something. Throughout history, the human race has mustered all its cleverness to defy the hostile forces of the weather and the dangers of life. Through precautions and plans, through pre-emptive action, dangers can be reduced and life made possible. For example by building a house. It protects us from the weather. Thus, we become less dependent. A house is the absolute epitome of all our endeavours, of technology and cleverness. And we all know something about building, even if the houses we build are not made of stone.

At the personal level, for example, we are constantly preoccupied with bringing our lives safely under cover. On a larger scale, we are working at making our social environment more homely and hospitable. Be it our country or the common European house - we are always building some sort of house for ourselves and for others. And that is good and important. So that we can resist dangers and facilitate lives, so that we can have something to set against the wind and the weather, fate and death. But we realise nonetheless that all this always remains under threat. Have we really got enough to set against the onslaught of the weather? Will the walls withstand the pressure? Will what we have done suffice, our personal and our joint efforts, our social and scientific constructions? Or is life on earth heading for disaster and collapse anyway?

192

The parable that Jesus tells addresses these questions. It presents two options to us: falling or standing firm. And it invites us to get to the bottom of these two options. Jesus wants us to look at the foundation. This is evidently not about superficial matters."

With this meditative introduction centred around the two words weather and house and all that we associate with them, the preacher has presented the hearers with a wide range of concepts with a view to enable them to identify with the sermon content; as a result, different hearers can get actively involved in the preaching process. By uncovering deeper layers underneath seemingly superficial everyday observations and events and thus addressing topics relevant to the lives of his hearers, he achieves two things: he reaches agreement with the hearers at the relationship level and makes them curious to find out what will come next at the subject level, particularly with regard to the biblical text:

Identifying with the sermon

"It is precisely because we are often in danger of remaining stuck at the surface, of getting entangled in the details or being overwhelmed by the abundance of tasks that lie ahead that we should, for once, not immediately focus on the deeds and works. Our lives do not flourish in doing and worrying. Jesus asks the fundamental question: What are our lives built upon? And he himself gives us the answer: God is the foundation of our lives. It is in him that we can stand firm and secure. God is the rock on which I can build the house of my life. His faithfulness is the basis for all our building endeavours. With this revelation, Jesus gives us a very important direction. If you (Jesus says) ask for God - in the midst of all the vicissitudes of life - then do not look up, but down! Do not look up, where the weather takes its ever-changing course. Don't search there! For God is not "the man up there" who rules over us arbitrarily, as unpredictable and moody as the weather. God does not change with the weather. No, that is not our God! He is not some weather deity. Not a god for fine weather. Neither is he a god who fires down thunderbolts at us. When the winds beat against your house, don't look for God in the storm. And even when the sun smiles down on you, that still isn't God. And when you hear everyone talking about God like about the weather, then know: God is not up there, but down in the deep. The very basis of your life. That which keeps

193

the house of your life secure in every weather, the rock, the foundation, the unmoveable base in the deep: that is God. What Jesus says is not unfounded. After all, he himself is the foundation. God down there, God in the deep, God with us in the midst of all the dangers we face and the efforts we make, that is Jesus Christ himself. He himself is the foundation on which we build. He in whom words and deeds came together in a unique unity. One who practised what he professed. One in whom God's faithfulness regarding his word and his promises became tangible. Precisely in the deep, even to death. That is why he is not being presumptuous by declaring his words the basis of our lives. It is on this foundation that we should build. Then we are truly wise. 'Everyone who hears these words of mine and puts them into practice is like a wise man ...' What makes us become wise? Wise is the one who hears."

d) The appeal aspect of preaching

Processing appeals

Appeals are aimed at effecting change in the lives of people. A preacher who calls for change must reckon with an in-built reluctance on the part of many hearers, which stems to a large degree from the circumstances surrounding their lives.[30] Homiletic research has shown that hearers will first take in what they can fit into the boundaries of their lives and conceptions without too much effort. Any appeals and messages that go beyond these boundaries will initially disturb their "inner domestic peace"[31] and will only be permanently received if the hearer is in a receptive frame of mind ("I am willing to have God and his preacher tell me something ..."). The preacher can (and should) of course only influence this inner attitude to a very limited extent. Moreover, our everyday experience teaches us that the road from a change in attitude to a change in behaviour can sometimes be long! If we consider how far our sermons reach we can easily become discouraged. Often our preaching appears to have little or

---

30 The psychologist I. Langer notes: "With every appeal you are entering a kingdom!" In order to defend this kingdom, people have developed a whole series of avoidance and defence strategies; some – even within churches – literally suffer from an "appeal allergy".

31 In psychology, the term *cognitive dissonance* is used to denote messages that we perceive as an "annoyance".

no effect. Many preachers long for experiences like those recorded in the Book of Acts (2:37): "When the people heard this, they were cut to the heart and said to Peter and the other apostles, "Brothers, what shall we do?"

Yet still today, people have such tangible experiences: a sermon helps them back on their feet, gives them joy and new heart. Or they commit their lives and affairs to God by consciously saying yes to Jesus' call: "Repent and believe the good news" (Mk. 1:15). Finally, people can permanently change the way they live their lives as a result of preaching and dedicate **Change** them in the name of the gospel to defending the interests of the **requires** weak and disadvantaged. Many developments and changes take **time** considerable time. The preacher is therefore urged to exercise patience and to display an "optimism of grace" (Gordon Rupp) and encouraged not to give up on making appeals.[32]

What is especially important to us in this context is to stress the opportunities of preaching while at the same time painting a realistic picture of what preaching can accomplish and what it **We only** cannot - particularly where it makes justified demands on the **achieve** hearers. The same principle applies as in the appeal aspect of **what we** communication discussed earlier: A person who does not want to **want to** achieve anything will not achieve anything. A preacher who does **achieve** not have a goal in mind with their sermon should not be surprised if it does not reach a goal. From the theological side, we are reminded that preachers follow in the biblical tradition of the prophets. They therefore explicitly have the right - and the duty! - "to interfere with internal affairs" (Manfred Fischer)! Especially lay preachers but also full-time ministers of the gospel sometimes perceive this as a burden. According to biblical tradition, a person who preaches speaks in the name of and on behalf of God. A person who preaches expects the Holy Spirit to work - both in themself and in the hearers. This knowledge alone can give the

---

32 In the same way that hearers may suffer from an appeal allergy, senders may have an "appeal phobia". Some preachers fear appeals, because they want to avoid coming across as authoritarian at all costs.

preacher the courage and calmness to include also the appellative aspect of the biblical message in their preaching.

Confirmation and contradiction, acceptance and correction all belong to preaching and must be balanced anew - both linguist**Accepting** ically and theologically - with every sermon. Thus, we can say: A **responsibility** person who preaches is responsible for what they say (and do not say). Neither the Holy Spirit nor the spirit of our times can be made responsible by the preacher for the effect of their sermon, if they have not managed to find the fertile middle ground between demanding too much and expecting too little of the congregation. The appellative aspect of preaching will therefore aim at effecting possible (!) changes in the hearers by making adequate demands on them while, at the same time, respecting their freedom and independence. They will then decide - whether we like it or not - what they will embrace in their lives and what they will reject. And finally: The most effective appeals in preaching are those that are expressed overtly and unambiguously - appeals that are responded to first in the preacher's own life. In doing so, the preacher signals at the relationship level: I do not expect anything of you that I am not willing to do myself!

We will now take a final look at our example to see how the preacher coveys the appeal aspects of the text.

"Wise is the one who hears. That is what gives our lives a foundation, a purpose. Listening out for the basis for our actions. Listening to the words of Jesus. That takes time ... What is, in actual fact, the basis for my actions. What reasons do I give for what I do? The way I interact with my children, for example, or the way I behave at work, what I do with my money? Whereby do I orientate myself, when I act consciously, and whereby, when I act spontaneously? As the East German author Christa Wolf looked at the crumbling façades of the monumental buildings shortly after the fall of the Berlin Wall (1989), she thought about the reasons for the collapse of communism in her country. She came to the conclusion that it was "an undisputed Lord to whom everything belonged, who supremely ruled over my city: the ruthless momentary advantage". So it is not the secret police or the political authorities that are to blame, but the ruthless

momentary advantage of every individual that made all this possible. Could it be that someone is holding up a mirror to us all? ... It is the preacher of the Sermon on the Mount, who recommends that we should accept disadvantages, setbacks, the long route, all for the sake of love. He is concerned with a consideration for others that lasts. Because it is love that has future and last for eternity.

Wise is the one who hears. And: Wise is the one who acts! A person who builds on the foundation of Jesus can build. And we can and must participate in building the house; we must invest all our wisdom to protect our world and its people from the small and the major climatic disasters. To hear and to do, that is what Jesus demands of us. It may be difficult from a theological point of view to work out the relationship between hearing and doing, believing and acting. And some may sense that so much call to action and the apostle Paul are sure to clash, sooner or later. However, even Paul makes it clear that the outcome must be action for the world. Not to act would be sin. But our relationship with God, the foundation of our house, is not called into question by what we build and how we build it. The relationship with the foundation remains. That is encouraging, even when it comes to doing something temporal. There are so many who need perfect conditions before they can begin. Often, however, we are required to build on the incomplete house, to plant the apple tree, even if we fear that the world will one day perish. Just to do what we have come to realise through our faith, even though it may be little. It is the basis, underlying motive that matters, and the goal: standing firm in the storms of life.

Wise is therefore also the one who does not judge quickly. Not everything that stands today will remain standing. Not everything that has fallen will remain cast away. The story of the fall of socialism, and of the free that is built on the rock - this is not the same story that is written in the bible. The fact that some can't help making this connection is understandable and has to do with our desire to always be right, to be found on the right side. Yet Jesus is definitely not concerned with this human desire to be right. Instead, he is concerned with God's justice, his law and our righteousness that should fulfil it. Whether our common house of Germany is built on sand, and will some day fall, or whether it is built on the rock has not yet been decided. But we have a part in this decision. And once again the question will be:

197

are we led by the ruthless momentary advantage, or are we willing to share in the long-term task by carrying one another's burdens and in this way fulfilling the law of Christ (Gal. 6:2). This is the principle behind today's collection for the solidarity campaign 'Carry each others burdens'. 'Everyone who hears these words of mine and puts them into practice is like a wise man - and has not built on sand.' Amen."

e) Looking back and looking ahead

In several steps, we considered the various aspects of communicating the gospel, particularly through preaching, from the perspective of communication studies. The purpose of this discussion was to show that the various factors involved in any communicative event are closely connected with one another. For this reason, there may be tension between the various aspects. With respect to the content aspect, for example, the following issues remain: Some topics cannot be adequately covered in a sermon of 15-20 minutes. Or the "repertoire of signs" in the language of the preacher is so different from that of the unchurched hearer who happens to walk into church that there is no understanding between the two. In the area of self-disclosure and relationship, significant differences in the basic positions of the preacher and the congregation (theological background, acceptance of societal developments, goals) may create serious tensions. In which direction should the appeal go in such a situation? Should the preacher and the congregation keep a graveyard peace or should the preacher continue with their appeal for the sake of "honesty" at all costs to the point of open conflict.

A common basis The above examples show: Without an amicable middle ground, a common basis, the relationship between the congregation and the preacher (whether in a full-time or a lay capacity) will not work for very long. A joint "quest for truth" (Gerd Theißen), which may even take the form of a "loving struggle" (Karl Jaspers), is a sign that people are getting involved in the process of spreading the kingdom of God with their own means and limitations as they put their confidence in God's promises. This is what the communication of the gospel is all about!

198

Chapter 8: Communicative preaching: concrete issues and examples

If we look at the proclamation of the Word of the bible from the perspective of communication research we will have to con- **Considering** sider not only the sermon, but also the environment in which it is **the sermon's** preached.[1] There will always be factors that are beyond the **environment** preacher's influence, such as the church building, the room, and the make-up of the congregation. From the perspective of communication studies, however, the propagation of the gospel is most likely to be successful where there is maximum agreement between inner and outer factors, and verbal and non-verbal factors.

In this final chapter, we will show by way of three concrete examples what communicative preaching means. We will begin by discussing the use of the first person ("I"- form) in the sermon. This will be followed by a discussion on the use of symbols in preaching. Finally, we will comment on a very serious topic, humour in the church and the pulpit.

I. Personal preaching: some thoughts regarding the use of "I" in the pulpit

"I believed; therefore I have spoken." These words were written by the apostle Paul in his second letter to the Corinthian **To convince,** church (2 Cor. 4:13); indeed, the vivacity of Paul's theological **we must be** writings stems from the very fact that they make reference to the **convinced** person who is behind their message, who knows deep inside that this message is the foundation of his life. This is an example of the basic human experience that we must be convinced of something ourselves if we want to convince others. At the same time, we can see that truth cannot be conveyed objectively, but will always contain a personal perspective. In his preaching and his epistles, Paul has the courage to speak as a person, although he makes his own role in relation to the communication of the gospel very clear, by saying: "We do not preach ourselves, but Jesus

---

1 Cf. explanation in chapter 1.

Christ as Lord, and ourselves as your servants for Jesus' sake." (2 Cor. 4:5)

Throughout the history of preaching the question of the "I" in the pulpit (i.e. the self-disclosure aspect in preaching) has been answered in a variety of ways during different eras and by different schools of theological thought. There have been and still are homiletics manuals that instruct aspiring preachers to preach nothing but the biblical text. The "I" in the sermon is only tolerated, at best, as an attesting "I"; otherwise, the afore-mentioned Pauline statement is cited: "We do not preach ourselves!" The other extreme is to demand authenticity in every case, as our preaching is strongly influenced by our own beliefs (our God image; our world view) and our own experiences. These two approaches each emphasise one particular claim, which is right in itself and cannot therefore be dismissed. However, regarding the first position, we may question whether "the text" (which, after all, also conveys its own story to specific hearers of that particular time) can really be related convincingly to today's hearers without conveying something of the person of the preacher and their story. The second position, on the other hand, may result in the biblical message being filtered through the preacher's own experience and knowledge of the world and consequently in a dangerous subjectivism. The biblical text will always have more to offer than our own subjective experience: the liberating, guiding Word which I cannot tell myself, which must come to me as a promise from outside.

The preacher as the second hearer In chapter 1, we said that God was the first hearer of the sermon; consequently, the preacher will be the second hearer of the sermon. As there can be no theological existence and no interpersonal communication without the person of the preacher, preachers should be encouraged to disclose something about themselves as well in their sermons. This does not necessarily mean talking about oneself all the time: "The fact that the preacher says 'I' and continually revolves around his own personal perceptions and shares his emotions with the hearers does not

200

make a sermon authentic; it is authentic if he expresses in clear terms that for which he can honestly accept responsibility."[2]

Preachers who decide, in the course of "that for which he can honestly accept responsibility," to say "I" will find Manfred Josuttis' differentiation of various uses of "I" in the sermon helpful:[3]

- The verifying (attesting) "I". Preachers use their own **The** Christian experience to attest to the message of the biblical text: **verifying "I"** "I have had the same experience as the apostle Peter that ..."
- The confessing "I". The preacher states agreement or **The** disagreement: "I am of a totally different (or: exactly the same) **confessing** opinion ..." Here, stating one's own position is not about **"I"** attesting the truth of the text by way of one's own experience (as in the previous variant), but to show, in one's own life, the variance between the God's truth and the reality of our existence.
- The bibliographical "I". Here, preachers share of their own person through their biography. They include childhood **The** experiences, encounters, or something they read that deeply **biographical** affected them, without trying to prove the legitimacy of the **"I"** truth of the biblical text through them. Thus, the preacher can - without undue exhibitionist tendencies - lead the hearers by way of their own life experience into the deep dimensions of human existence.
- The representative "I". The preacher speaks about self without referring to their own biography. Instead, speaking of self on **The** behalf of all the hearers. Thus they seek to approach the text in **representative** a way that is personal, yet at the same time and applicable to all. **"I"** The use of this form of "I" makes it possible for the hearers to identify strongly with the preacher. The problem of this "I"-form lies in its tendency to "take over" the hearers, especially if the representative "I" (which is not easily recognisable to the hearers) is combined with a confessing "I".

2   H. M. Müller, Homiletik, Berlin/New York 1996, p. 291.
3   Cf. M. Josuttis, Praxis des Evangeliums zwischen Politik und Religion, Munich 1974, pp. 70-94.

The exemplary "I"

- The exemplary "I" is very similar to the representative "I". Again, the preacher uses their own person to convey to the hearers what is important to them as well. Yet, the exemplary form makes it clear that the preacher hears the text initially for themself, and only after having heard it, they discuss its meaning for the hearers.

The fictitious "I"

- The fictitious "I". Like a novel, a sermon may feature an imaginary "I" that is clearly not identical with the preacher. Many passages of scripture can be retold or even preached from an "I"- perspective. It is then King David, the prophet Jonah, or Mary the mother of Jesus who share from their experiences with God. Job unfolds his doubts and his misery, or one of the women who met the risen Christ allows the hearers to share in her Easter joy, which is still mingled with fear ...

The demanding "I"

We can extend this list by adding two more "I"- forms: the demanding and the claiming "I". Both these variants occur mainly in challenging discourse (cf. chapter 3). In political or evangelistic sermons, the preacher demands something of their hearers or declares facts to them, without making a connection with her own religious experience. This reveals a normative assertion of the preacher, which she believes to have on the basis of her calling and appointment to the preaching ministry. This normative assertion may either be accepted by the hearers as God given authority, or rejected as pretentious.

The above list shows the multifarious linguistic possibilities in which the person of the preacher may feature in the preaching of

"We"-statements

the word in the "I"-form. In this context, we need to take a brief look at the use of the "we"-form. "We" should be used in the sermon even more cautiously than "I"! The advantage of "we"-statements lies in the fact that they create a genuine sense of togetherness between the preacher and the hearers and express this togetherness in a word. The danger of the "we"-form lies in the possibility of "taking over" the hearers (false "we").

However, if preachers use neither the "I" - form nor the "we"-form they run the risk that the hearers will perceive the sermon as being impersonal and distant. Without the use of the first person ("I"/"we"), preachers will not easily be able to find statements that include them and the hearers, jointly standing before God as addressees of the sermon.

II. Illustrative preaching: the use of symbols in the sermon

1. THE LANGUAGE OF IMAGES AS THE MOTHER TONGUE OF FAITH

The girl stood on the shore
And heaved a heavy sigh.
It made her kinda sore
To watch the sunset die.

Hey baby don't you frown,
It happens all the time:
The sun goes down in front
Then pops up from behind.

This poem by the German writer Heinrich Heine (1797-1856) illustrates the difference between a purely practical and a symbolic perspective of the same thing.[4] Which perspective is right? Probably both, each in its own way. Nowadays, every child knows that the earth rotates and that sunsets are the result of this rotation. Yet no one ever says: "Look at how beautifully the earth is rotating!", but rather, "What a beautiful sunset!" Beside the mere explanation of facts we have a deeper symbolic perspective. Depending on the situation and the person concerned, either one will dominate over the other when truth is expressed.

The Old Testament is full of true-to-life metaphoric language. Thus, for example, the Hebrew word for soul *(nefesh)* is based on the root word for "throat", the essential place for food intake and inhalation. In important passages, we also find a close connection between speech and symbolic action, especially in the prophetic

---

4   H. Heine, Sämtliche Werke, ed. by E. Elster, Vol.1, Leipzig/Vienna 1889, p. 229 (transl. by Doug Robinson).

writings of the Hebrew bible. In the book of Isaiah, for instance, the people of Israel is referred to by means of the speaking image of "God's vineyard" (Is. 5:1ff). At Yahweh's command, Jeremiah (Jer. 27:2) puts a wooden yoke on his shoulders to reinforce his prophecy concerning the yoke of Nebuchadnezzar. Ezekiel runs through the city with his belongings packed for exile in order to underline his message (Ez. 12:1ff). In the case of Hosea, the prophet's wife and children are involved in the prophetic assignment - in a way that is hardly conceivable to us today (Hos. 1:2ff).

In the New Testament, it is not much different. Jesus constantly used comparisons and metaphors, puns and symbols in his preaching. He used everyday things as a starting point for telling his hearers about God within the context of their world (with their reality and their logic). It is only in this light that we can really understand, for example, the parables of the sower (Mk. 4:1-20a), the mustard seed (Mk. 4:30-34a), the lost sheep, the lost coin, or the two sons who were both lost, each in his own way (Lk. 15). In the same way, the metaphorical "I ams" of John's gospel appeal to the understanding and the reality of the people of the biblical era. All these examples show: "Jesus introduced gestures, symbols, illustrations of the new life and established new meanings ... He not only created friendship but also new expressions of this friendship, making them an example for us: bread and wine, oil and water, blessings and embraces, foot washing and writing in the sand, fasting and drinking all became new gestures of life."[5]

These symbols of life, as we find them in the bible, have been interpreted and employed in a variety of ways throughout church history. For centuries, post-Reformation homiletics with its emphasis on the word was largely "homiletics without symbols" (Horst Albrecht). In contrast, Orthodox and Roman Catholic traditions have for some time been more open to the use of symbols in preaching and homiletics. Over the past three decades,

---

5   F. Steffensky, Feier des Lebens, Spiritualität im Alltag, Stuttgart 1984, p.78.

204

Protestants too have begun to pay more attention to the use of symbols in both biblical teaching and preaching from the pulpit. Besides the educational reasons resulting from social changes[6], this new openness to the use of symbols is mainly due to a theological realisation. The purpose of the communication of the gospel in all its various manifestations is to speak of God, to express that which cannot be said, to depict that which cannot be depicted. This is can only be achieved through metaphoric and symbolic language. When speaking of the absolute and the ultimate, the holy and the eternal, we cannot do without symbols. Thus, the language of symbols may be regarded as the "mother tongue of faith". Speaking of the "purpose and the right of religious symbols", the theologian Paul Tillich wrote:

To talk about God, we need symbols

"Religious symbols need no justification if their purpose is clear. Their purpose is that they are the language of the religions, the only language by which religion can be directly expressed. We can make statements *about* religion using philosophical and theological terms, or we can try to grasp the religious through art. Yet, the religious itself can only find expression in symbols or in complexes of symbols which - when combined into a unit - we refer to as myths."[7]

The use of symbols in this context is not merely about giving illustrations in the sense of superficially increasing the hearers' attentiveness. This will become clear as we consider some of the characteristics of religious symbols, exemplified by the symbol of water.

Characteristics of religious symbols

---

6   Examples attesting to this include: (1) our increasingly multifarious society makes it more difficult to interpret the correlations of life. (2) The number of people who have any biblical knowledge, which could serve as a basis for Christian preaching and teaching, is steadily decreasing. (3) Educational processes are never completed and must not be limited to imparting intellectual knowledge.

7   Sinn und Recht religiöser Symbole, in: P. Tillich, Symbol und Wirklichkeit, 3rd Ed., Göttingen 1986, p.3.

2. FIVE CHARACTERISTICS OF RELIGIOUS SYMBOLS

a) Symbols are part of the finite reality and point beyond it

Symbols are words, pictures, objects, and actions with more than one meaning. They are, so to speak, translucent for a reality that lies behind everyday reality. The visible becomes transparent so the invisible can be seen. Symbols are part of the finite reality and, at the same time, point beyond it. Conversely, we can say: while they have a figurative meaning, it must always be possible to understand them literally as well.[8] Besides the obvious aspect that

Additional symbolic aspect can be described with the means of the exact sciences, there is an additional symbolic aspect. This additional aspect is, so to speak, consolidated in the symbol. That explains the meaning of the word: the Greek *symballein* may be translated as "to throw together", or "to unite".

Example: Water. In an encyclopaedia, we would find the following factual information under the entry "water": "tasteless, odourless liquid, colourless in shallow amounts, the oxide of hydrogen, melting point 0°, boiling point 100° ..."[9] which describes water from a scientific point of view as an essential element of life. A look at the semantic field of the word "water" will reveal the abundance of meanings associated with this symbol: water-power, water pollution, holy water, water shortage, waterfall, flood water, troubled water, waterway, to water, etc.

b) Symbols are part of the infinite reality to which they point

Symbols often express things that are beyond words, things that can only be sensed or imagined. Symbols stand for realities

Mysteries remain mysteries that are greater than we are. They bring us into contact with realities that we do not fully know, that will always remain unfathomable, no matter how much we try. Symbols unveil mysteries to us; yet these mysteries remain mysteries even after they have become "known". This applies especially to matters of faith.

---

8 This distinguishes them from metaphors, which are to be understood always in the figurative sense.

9 Das neue Fischer Lexikon in Farbe, Vol. 10, Munich 1981, p. 387.

Let us look again at the example of water. The sentence "Without water there can be no life!" is true in a variety of ways: first in the literal sense and then in the figurative sense. The symbol of a spring reminds us that, even in times of drought, there is hope for life. The symbol of a river points to the fact that nothing is stagnant: "everything flows! - even our lives flow in a continuous cycle of being born, growing, and passing away. The big wide ocean reminds us of the things that may lie hidden below the surface of our lives: the treasures that must be raised and the burdens that must be buried forever in the deep.

As an essential resource of life, water also reminds us of mankind's responsibility to preserve the basis of life, and of the blessing of God on which all life on earth depends every day anew. Thus, God is referred to in the Old Testament as the "fountain of life" (Ps. 36:9). For Christians, water is also a reminder of baptism in the name of the triune God who, being the creator, the sustainer, and perfecter of the cosmos, manifests his grace to the individual in the person of Jesus Christ.

c) Symbols have a "life": they are born and they die

Mere signs, such as road signs or characters of the alphabet, can be invented, introduced and abolished. They do not necessarily have to have anything to do with the content for which they stand. Symbols, in contrast, are tied to their content. As substitutes, they have a kind of life story; "they are born and they die" (Paul Tillich). A Symbol may sink into oblivion or once again emerge to become topical; its meaning is not fixed forever. **Symbols are tied to their content**

The example of water: throughout the ages and in all human cultures, water has always been a symbol for religious statements and rituals of faith. Thus, water may be regarded as a symbol with a high constancy. As a result of the recent destruction of our environment, the meaning of water as a symbol of life is becoming increasingly prominent again. The more people are conscious in their everyday lives of their complete dependency on water, the stronger the symbolic charge of the word will be reflected in the area of their faith.

The bible contains a near endless number of references to water with a wide range of meanings. In the first account of the Creation, the Spirit of God is described as "hovering over the waters" of the chaos (Gen. 1:2f). In God's new world, all who are thirsty may take the free gift of "the water of life" (Rev. 22:17). For the witnesses of the bible, the connection of water with judgement and grace would have been very plausible, as it reflected their everyday experience. This explains the frequent use of the symbol, particularly in fundamental theological concepts.

d) Symbols convey the meaning of reality, particularly where this is not possible through other means.

Variety of meanings
Our everyday world is determined to a large extent by ideas and behavioural patterns which are based on economic interests and the natural sciences. Logical thinking in the sense of cause and effect takes pre-eminence over everything else. Due to their variety of meanings, symbols are capable of drawing our attention to deeper realities that otherwise lie buried under the surface of mere factual contexts. They are effective where the intellect reaches its limits. They appeal to the whole person, they "give us something to think about" (Paul Ricoeur), but also something to feel and to understand more deeply. This applies especially to religious symbols. Thus, holy writings and pictures, or an encounter in a holy place allow us to partake of the holy itself, yet without it being at our disposal. However, even if we venture a symbolic interpretation of everyday events, we will - often unexpectedly - discover amazing clues regarding the mystery of our world and the meaning of life. This may apply to the individual, a particular community of people, or the world as a whole.

The example of water: We drink water; we use it to prepare food, to clean our bodies, to wash our clothes. We use water in our daily routine, usually without giving it much thought. It often takes a disruption of the usual (natural or environmental disaster, a burst pipe) to make us realise how precious every single drop of water really is.

On the one hand, the symbol of water reminds us of our dependency as individual human beings, on the other hand, it helps us to recognise larger contexts in the following areas:

- the *social* ("Bread and water") - a symbol for punishment for committing a crime)
- the *economic* ("share" or "allocation of water"? - this addresses the issue of justice)
- the *political* (as the most important natural resource of the 21st century, water may be the cause of conflicts and armed hostilities)
- and the *religious* (constant dependency of all life on factors that are beyond human control).

e) The effects of symbols are ambivalent

According to Tillich, symbols have "power to edify, to order, to subvert, and to destroy".[10] This is true of individuals and the community alike. As varied as the symbols are, they can affect us in very different ways. The function of a symbol is determined **Symbols** largely by its acceptance and use within a given community. In **must be** the early days of Christendom, for example, the symbol of the **accepted** fish[11] quickly became the sign by which Christians would recognise each other. This symbol could only spread throughout Christianity, because people experienced spiritual fellowship and social care in the name of Christ in the churches and supported one another in times of need.

At this point, we have to warn of a danger in the use of symbols: Human experience and world history show that **Symbols** individuals, images, and objects can be built up into idols and **can be** used as a means for inhumane propaganda and destruction. **abused**

---

10 P. Tillich, loc. cit., p. 5.
11 The Greek word for fish *(ichthys)* was used as an abbreviation for Jesus Christ God's Son and Saviour.

The example of water: as we encounter it in various forms (as a gas, a liquid, and a solid), water is also a symbol of the amorphous, and of adaptation and transformation. In the form of a glassy lake, water can radiate calm and peace; in the form of the raging sea it can represent the coldness of the power of death. The symbol of fresh spring water can release energy. The sunset over the sea can keep the yearning for life and freedom alive in us. In the same way, the symbols of a sun baked river bed or a dried-up well can destroy all hope of life and a future. We also find the multifarious effects of the symbol of water in the bible. Rain is the symbol of bestowed blessings (Ps. 65:11). However, in the account of the flood, it is also a symbol of the judgement of God (Gen. 7:1ff), which - as expressed in the sign of the rainbow - should not be repeated again (Gen. 8,22). By turning water into wine, Jesus reveals himself as the friend of life (John 2:1-11). He uses water to wash his disciples' feet (John 13:5f); in baptism, people are united with him in his death and resurrection (Rom. 6).

This variety of effects found in the biblical accounts makes it impossible to interpret the symbol of water in one particular way. The meaning of the symbol, like the substance itself, remains fluid.

In summary: Symbols are meaning-carrying objects which are at home in our finite reality, but can be used to point beyond it. Religious symbols function as bridges between our everyday reality and the reality of God. Due to their surplus and elasticity of meaning, biblical symbols and symbols taken from the world around us are appropriate means to express the religious, without which an experience of faith can neither be grasped nor conveyed. Symbols appeal not only to the mind, but also to the emotions; they are aimed at the whole person. As symbols are situationally determined and ambiguous, it is necessary to have some guidelines for interpretation or a hermeneutic key in order to ensure successful communication.[12]

The need for interpreting guidelines

---

12 Paul, for example, uses the term "word of the cross" (1 Cor. 1:18) as a criterion for an adequate understanding of the gospel message.

3. FIVE RULES FOR USING SYMBOLS IN THE SERMON

First, we can differentiate four categories of symbols that occur both in the bible and in our present-day world: language, pictures, objects, and actions.

All four categories may be used in preaching:

- *Texts:* Biblical narratives and accounts, prayers (psalms), prophetic texts, doctrinal statements and creeds.[13] Liturgical texts and hymns. Poems, narratives from world literature and songs. Religious writings from various traditions. Current articles from daily papers and periodicals. **Texts**

- *Pictures:* Religious and secular paintings, graphic arts, prints and art postcards, photographs, slides, overhead projector acetates, films and videos, computer animations and presentations with the aid of a video beamer. **Pictures**

- *Objects:* Sacred objects and *objets d'art* found within the church (Cross/crucifix, bible, candles, baptismal font). Any objects brought along by the preacher, such as a clay pitcher, an old wagon wheel, a floppy disk, a flower bulb. **Objects**

- *Actions:* Sacred acts in baptism and Holy Communion. Symbolic gestures, such as laying-on of hands for blessing, anointing with oil, crossing, often in connection with special events (e.g. baptism, confirmation, marriage, funeral). Performing elements in the propagation of the gospel, such as drama, pantomime, dance, symbolic actions, processions, silent marches. **Actions**

As the above examples show, not every option is suitable for every preaching situation and every preacher. In all cases, the preacher must ensure coherence with the sermon, because not everything is sanctified by its association. The following rules have proved helpful when using symbols and objects in preaching:

---

13 In the early days of the formation of Christian doctrines the creeds were referred to as symbols.

a) Focusing on a symbol, in a world of symbols

Concentrating on the essential

If we assume that symbols touch people in their innermost being we should ensure that we do not create a muddle of many different symbols, but rather concentrate on one symbol and its symbolic world. A deeper understanding of the symbol can only be achieved if distracting and disrupting factors are eliminated as far as possible. Now, a surfeit of symbols may actually cause the hearers to become distracted instead of helping them to concentrate on the essential. Nowadays, the situation is aggravated by the fact that we have to cope with an inflation of symbols, for it is not only in church that symbols are used. The advertising industry and the electronic media have also discovered the power of the symbolic. In particular the religious symbols are being used (the cross, modified bible quotations, persons dressed in church garments). Trend researcher Matthias Horx states: "The more society turns away from church, the more common religious symbols become in popular culture."[14]

Less is more

If we want to regain lost Christian symbols for our church activities, we must first and foremost apply the rule: less is more! It is only then that the precious can be recognised as being precious. This of course requires confidence on the preacher's part that the symbol will convey its message.

In his standard work on the use of symbols in teaching published in 1982, the Roman Catholic religious educationalist Hubertus Halbfas voiced sharp criticism of the "thematic problem-orientated religious education" that was prevalent at the time. His admonition regarding the appropriate use of symbols in preaching and teaching still applies:

"What we have been left with is unrefined. All kinds of media are used to the point of overkill. They are no longer carefully explored step by step in respect of their own message; instead a set of predetermined thematic questions is answered. That way, texts, pictures, films, and audiotapes are abused as mere 'pegs', 'visual aids', 'materials for discussion', 'examples for

---

14 M. Horx, Trendbuch II, 2nd Ed., Düsseldorf 1996, p. 123.

application', while often being deprived of the dignity of having their own meanings. The most shameful example of this is the way in which biblical texts are used as an alibi for discussing a particular issue. As a result, these 'media' are employed in a thematic functional manner: general perspectives, vague clichés, and sweeping statements prevail. The diligent search for deeper meanings and nuances, for gentle whispers and the unutterable has become the exception."[15]

b) Introducing the symbol

In our fast and ever-changing world, we need to reduce the stimuli to our senses if we want to deal with symbols in a deeper **Reducing** way. We will not be in touch with our innermost being in passing **the stimuli** quickly and especially not on command. Preachers should **to our** therefore not simply thrust a symbol upon the hearers, but **senses** gradually introduce them to it. This can be done already when welcoming the congregation to the service, by saying (a few!) linking words in between the scripture readings, but especially in the sermon itself. The preacher then takes their hearers step by step along the journey of the sermon and stop for a rest at suitable vantage points.

In the context of using symbols, it has proved useful to prepare the environment accordingly. Such preparation may include **A prepared** appropriate room decorations, purposeful seating arrangements, **environment** suitable music, etc. The purpose is to get the attention of the hearers and help them to focus. Experience shows that this can best be attained in an atmosphere of silent reflection.

For a sermon on the marriage at Cana (John 2:1-11) in which I discussed the topic "change is possible", I had some clay pitchers put in various places around the church. Beside the pulpit stood a thin pedestal. At the beginning of the sermon, I placed a large clay pitcher on this pedestal and, in a meditative manner, drew some connections between the symbol of the clay pitcher and human life. I then invited the hearers to connect inwardly with the symbol, by asking themselves questions like:

---

15 H. Halbfas, Das dritte Auge, Düsseldorf 1982, p.29.

213

What does the pitcher of my life look like? What is inside? By what might the pitcher of my life be threatened (hammer)? Has water ever been turned into wine in my life through God's working? Where is change required and what can I do myself to change?

In the course of the sermon, I brought out the promise of the biblical story: in God's presence change is possible.

c) Confidence in the symbol

Dealing with the symbol in a deeper way requires time. If the preacher progresses too quickly with the sermon the hearers may cease to think about the meaning of the symbol. It is also important for the preacher to trust that the symbol will speak for itself, or that it is taken into service by the Spirit of God. Rash, definitive explanations restrain the hearers in their thoughts and emotions. In contrast, careful, expectant moderation encourages them to actively assimilate the content of the symbol.

The use of symbols in preaching appeals especially to the hearers' imagination. Any minor divergence from the anticipated (e.g. applying the symbol within an unusual context) will normally recapture the hearers' attention. Stark contrasts (introducing a counter-symbol; destroying the symbol) provoke and open up new horizons of understanding to those who receive them. However, if we take this too far we must expect opposition on the part of the hearers.

d) Unintroducing the symbol

If we preach about the wedding at Cana we must not leave the hearers behind in Galilee. Preaching means making the journey from the here and now to the text, and back! Consequently, a responsible use of symbols entails accompanying the hearers back from their encounter with the symbol to everyday reality. If we fail to do this we run the risk that, in the end, everything will remain as it was. Then the Sunday morning church service would be of no significance for everyday Christian service (Rom. 12:1).

One purpose of accompanying the hearers on their journey back to everyday life is to make them aware of the limitations of **The** their encounter with the symbol. On the one hand, it is clear that **limitations** no text, picture, or symbol is capable of saying everything, nor **of symbols** does it have to say everything. On the other hand, some symbols can trigger quite different or even contrary trains of thought. If such ambiguous symbols are used in preaching without any qualifications they can cause the interpretation of the sermon content to become arbitrary. This may occur, for example, in the case of a stone, which may be both a positive symbol for steadfastness and perpetuity and a negative symbol for coldness and violence. We must therefore ask ourselves how this symbol **Symbol** must be interpreted within the framework of the gospel, or more **criticism** precisely: how it relates to the pivotal symbol of Christianity, the cross. Furthermore, the preacher must consider what prospects may result from the encounter with the symbol for both the individual and the community as a whole.

There are several ways in which a symbol that has been introduced can be unintroduced again. This can be achieved in the sermon itself: in the case of the above example, by saying farewell to Cana. The hearers may be asked to write what they gained from the service on a piece of paper and thus take it home with them in black and white. Or the preacher suggests how that which was said and experienced in the service might affect his/her own life or the lives of the hearers over the coming days and weeks.

Another way of unintroducing symbols is by inviting personal contributions from individual hearers in which they relate personal faith experiences relating to the symbol. Experiences with the symbol may also be brought before God in the intercessory prayers.

e) Securing the harvest

The propagation of the gospel occurs under the promise of God. We may therefore expect God to give his people a deep, life changing understanding when they reflect on the biblical word and the symbols related to it. The fact that this understanding will also

Reminding and reiterating prove its power in everyday life is also a spiritual process. We are by no means disputing this, when we draw attention to the psychological realisation that symbols (especially objects) serve to reiterate what is said and help the hearers to remember it. Learning psychology research has proved that the average person will retain less than 20% of what has merely been heard. If the hearing is accompanied by seeing, this figure increases to more than 50%. 70% of what a person says will normally remain in his/her memory. If seeing and speaking are accompanied by doing, the figure rises above 90%.[16] Thus it would make sense when using the learning psychology model (cf. chapter 4) to add a consolidation phase after the solution phase.

Suggestions for action An example of this might be to give each member of the congregation a copy of the symbol used in the sermon (e.g. miniature clay pitcher: "Change is possible - John 2:1-11)" at the end of the service to take home as a reminder. If the hearer then keeps looking at the little clay pitcher, for example on his/her desk, it will serve to reiterate the sermon content. One could even go further by suggesting concrete action in the sermon to be realised in the form of a project. Examples of this might be:

- setting up a play group at a nearby playground
- carrying out a neighbourhood project together with other Christians in the area
- forming a partnership with a church in a foreign country

Conclusion: In the above, we discussed the possibilities of using symbols in preaching. In doing so, we showed the limitations of this endeavour. Symbols should by no means be looked upon as a cure-all for the believers' speechlessness, which is often lamented. Nonetheless, the language of symbols, the mother tongue of faith, is indispensable for communicating of the gospel with the purpose of attesting God's presence in the world in a relevant and comprehensible way.

---

16 Cf. K. Witzenbacher, Praxis der Unterrichtsvorbereitung, Munich 1994.

III. Preaching with humour: laughing is good for you - and for the sermon!

A vicar tells his colleague, "I've got a problem with bats in my church. I've tried everything, but I just can't get rid of them. Have you got any suggestions what I could do?" The colleague replies, "Oh yes, I have. I had the same problem. I simply christened and confirmed them, and I haven't seen them since."

Christianity, particularly Protestantism, is not exactly renowned for its humour. Friedrich Nietzsche expressed the criticism that can hardly be dismissed: "Better songs would they have to sing, for me to believe in their Saviour: more! Like saved ones would his disciples have to appear unto me!"[17] The reservations of many Christians when it comes to humour (in the context of faith, God and the church) appears to be paralleled in writings of the Old and the New Testament.[18]

We very rarely read in the Hebrew bible that God laughs; at best we hear him laugh in scorn in the light of human folly (cf. Ps. 2:37; Ps. 59:9). On the other hand, the Old Testament exhibits humour in its account of the naming of the great Jewish patriarch Isaac. The name Isaac (*Yitzhak*, Hebrew: he laughed) goes back to the story in Genesis (17:15-21 and 18:1-15) in which Abraham and Sarah are promised a son by God in their old age, and Sarah responds to this by laughing. Thus, one might say that laughter wrote Old Testament history, and indeed "Heilsgeschichte".

Laughter in the bible

In the New Testament, we do not find much either in respect of laughter.[19] While those that weep are promised in the beatitudes (Lk. 6:21) that they will laugh in the future, those who laugh now are warned a few verses later in the woes that they will mourn and

---

17 Von den Priestern, in: F. Nietzsche, Also sprach Zarathustra II (1883), Kritische Studienausgabe, Neuausgabe Munich 1999, p. 118 (transl. by Thomas Common).

18 We find very few instances of the genre joke in the bible (1 Sam. 21, 11-15; 2 Sam. 6:16 and 20-23; Gal. 5:20). Cf. W. Thiede, Das verheißene Lachen, Humor in theologischer Perspektive, Göttingen 1986.

19 Concerning humour as a whole, the reality is quite different, especially in the gospels of the New Testament. See: R. Buckner, The Joy of Jesus. Humour in the Gospels, Norwich 1993.

weep (Lk. 6:25). The Greek church father John Chrysostom claimed that Jesus never laughed. Werner Thiede explains the portrayal of a serious Jesus in the gospels by "the compassion which was characteristic of Jesus ... Jesus' compassion naturally puts him on the side of those who suffer as a result of their fellow human beings, disasters, hunger, sickness, death, and even God himself. His path is portrayed as a relentless path to the cross – his enemies were able to laugh, albeit a bitter laugh!"[20]

Laughter and faith   Although it is true that nothing is said explicitly in the scriptures, we may assume that the feast at the wedding of Cana (John 2: 1-10) was not a sad occasion. Moreover, at the end of the Sermon on the Mount, the gospel of Matthew relates a parable of Jesus about building a house in the figurative sense. If we take a closer look at this parable we will find that it has - like many parables –more than a hint of fine irony. Indeed, the synoptic gospels of the New Testament do include more humorous aspects than it may look like at first sight. Here we find quite a number of stories, parables and sayings in which Jesus uses various types of humour, ranging from pure absurdity to subtle irony, from riddles to amusing parables, from stating the obvious to using throwaway lines and catch phrases. Philosopher and theologian D. Elton Trueblood in his classic work "Humor of Christ" points out an often neglected aspect, the *universality* of Jesus' use of humour, its diversity and complexity; Trueblood's book provides an appendix identifying "Thirty Humorous Passages in the Synoptic Gospels"[21].

Even if there appears to be little in the bible to laugh about, one might suggest that the accounts of the joy of those that have been set free and of the rejoicing of the redeemed include humour

---

20 Loc. cit. p.40.
21 D. E. Trueblood, Humor of Christ, New York 1964/1990, p.127. Some
    inspiring examples of this list are: "No need to borrow trouble" (Matt. 6:34);
    "The good old wine" (Luke 5:39); "Whitewashed tombs" (Matt. 23:27);
    "Broad phylacteries" (Matt. 23:5), "Camel through needle's eye" (Matt.
    19:24, Mark 10:25, Luke 18:25).

and laughter.[22] The philosopher and Christian author Sören Kierkegaard made the following statement with reference to 1 John 5:4: "Humour is ... the joy that has overcome the world." The reason for a close inner relation between humour and faith is found in the fact that both have to do with the ambivalence of life. Faith has to deal with the ultimate questions of human existence and so can humour in its various forms. A well-chosen joke or a riddle are capable of speaking directly to our hearts and minds, a phrase or story of subtle irony can bear existential depth that makes us think for a while. Both faith and humour can show something of the human spirit's ability to extract from a given situation, and help us towards a new understanding of "reality" including its muddles and inconsistencies from a different perspective. Good humour wants to say something more than just "have fun!"; it makes people smile or laugh and at the same time it wants them to realize what is true and what needs to be said in order to initiate change.

Laughing establishes relationships and captures attention

The function of humour in preaching can also be more than merely providing "additional stimuli" to a well-designed speech as has been suggested by educationists, rhetoricians or communication psychologists. There's more to it because both humour and faith can highlight truth; a well-told story or parable may "say it all" and any further explanation may distract or dilute its content. As preachers of the gospel we are invited to follow Jesus' example by looking out for compelling stories and appropriate analogies, for contemporary parables and thought-provoking ironic phrases that illuminate aspects of truth like rays of light in a burning glass, so that our hearers may become involved personally with us in wondering about the one who says: "He/she who has ears to hear, let him/her hear" (Mark 4:9).

We have already suggested that in every church service there should be at least one opportunity to laugh. This suggestion is not

---

22 Cf. H. Cox, Das Fest der Narren. Das Gelächter ist der Hoffnung letzte Waffe, Berlin/Stuttgart 1970; J. Moltmann, Die ersten Freigelassenen der Schöpfung. Versuche über die Freude an der Freiheit und das Wohlgefallen am Spiel, 5th Ed., Munich 1976.

meant to contradict the seriousness of the church service and the sermon. Yet, we have surely all experienced that "redeeming laughter"[23] in response to a humorous remark or reaction helped to relieve a tense situation. It is far easier to get to the heart of a matter through a well-chosen caricature or an apt joke than through clinical analysis! Laughter, like smiling, is contagious and unites people; laughing creates a positive atmosphere for learning, laughter can draw attention to important things, also in the service and the sermon. Anyone who has initially laughed at a joke or a drama sketch and later realised, "You are the man (the woman)!" (cf. 2 Sam. 12:7) will be aware how effective and helpful humour can be particularly where criticism needs to be expressed. Learning from the bible at this point means to employ good humour in giving witness to - both God's and the preacher's - compassion, fellowship, serenity and love in our sermons. Those who like to use humour in preaching must be sensitive to the situation and atmosphere. It can be quite embarrassing if nobody laughs at your joke. The same guidelines apply to humour as to the use of stories and symbols. Carefully select, don't overdo, and use it appropriately!

Humour and criticism

---

23 This is the title of a book on the subject written by the American sociologist P. L. Berger, Berlin/New York 1997.

Bibliography

I. Source materials on homiletics/History of Preaching

- Beutel, Albrecht/Drehsen, Volker: Wegmarken protestantischer Predigtgeschichte, Tübingen 1999.
- Brilioth, Yngve: A Brief History of Preaching, Philadelphia 1965.
- Wilson, Paul Scott: A Concise History of Preaching, Nashville 1992.

II. Homiletic manuals/Textbooks/Theology of Preaching

- Allen, Ronald J: Preaching. An Essential Guide, Nashville 2002.
- Bohren, Rudolf: Predigtlehre, 5th Ed., Munich 1995.
- Buttrick, David: Homiletic. Moves and Structures, Philadelphia 1987.
- Craddock, Fred B: Preaching, Nashville 1985.
- Engemann, Wilfried: Einführung in die Homiletik, Tübingen/Basel 2002.
- English, Donald: An Evangelical Theology of Preaching, Nashville 1996.
- Eslinger, Richard L: The Web of Preaching. New Options in Homiletic Method, Nashville 2002
- Hirschler, Horst: Biblisch predigen, 3rd Ed., Hannover 1992.
- Lischer, Richard: A Theology of Preaching, Nashville 1981.
- Lowry, Eugene L: The Sermon. Dancing the Edge of Mystery, Nashville 1997.
- Massey, James E: The Burdensome Joy of Preaching, Nashville 1998.
- Müller, Hans Martin: Homiletik, Berlin/New York 1996.
- Wilson, Paul Scott: The Practice of Preaching, Nashville 1995.
- —, The Four Pages of the Sermon. A Guide to Biblical Preaching, Nashville 1999.

III. The language and rhetoric of preaching

- Cunningham, David: Faithful Persuasion. In Aid of a Rhetoric of Christian Theology, Notre Dame/London 1991.
- Grözinger, Albrecht: Die Sprache des Menschen, Munich 1991.
- Hauser, Gerard A: Introduction to Rhetorical Theory, Prospect Heights 1991.
- McClure, John S: The Four Codes of Preaching. Rhetorical Strategies, Minneapolis 1991.
- Otto, Gert: Rhetorische Predigtlehre, Leipzig 1999.

IV. Psychological aspects of preaching

- Engemann, Wilfried: Persönlichkeitsstruktur und Predigt, 2nd Ed., Berlin 1992.
- Schulz von Thun, Friedemann: Miteinander reden, 1–3, 3 Vols., Reinbek 1981, 1989, 1998.
- P. Watzlawick/J. H. Beavin/D. D. Jackson, Pragmatics of Human Communication. A Study of Interactional Patterns, New York 1967.

V. Church service and sermon

- Herbst, Michael/Schneider, Michael: Wir predigen nicht uns selbst. Ein Arbeitsbuch zur Predigt - und Gottesdienstvorbereitung, Neukirchen-Vluyn 2001.
- Schmidt-Lauber, Hans-Christoph/Karl-Heinrich Bieritz/Michael Meyer-Blanck (ed.): Handbuch der Liturgik. Liturgiewissenschaft in Theologie und Praxis der Kirche, 3rd rev. Ed., Göttingen 2003.
- Saliers, Don E: Worship as Theology. Foretaste of Glory Divine, Nashville 1994.
- Stookey, Laurence Hull: Calendar. Christ's Time for the Church, Nashville 1996.
- White, James F: Introduction to Christian Worship, 3rd rev. Ed., Nashville 2000.

VI. Women and Preaching/Justice/Cultural Aspects

- Atkins, Martyn D: Preaching in a Cultural Context, Peterborough 2001.
- Black, Kathy: A Healing Homiletic. Preaching and Disability, Nashville 1996.
- González, Justo L./González, Catherine G: The Liberating Pulpit, Nashville 1994.
- Jost, Renate/Schwaiger, Ulrike (ed.): Feministische Impulse für den Gottesdienst, Stuttgart 1996.
- Kurewa, John Wesley Zwomunondiita: Preaching and Cultural Identity. Proclaiming the Gospel in Africa, Nashville 2000.
- Mitchell, Henry H: Black Preaching. The Recovery of a Powerful Art, Nashville 1990.
- Norén, Carol M: The Woman in the Pulpit, Nashville 1991.
- Smith, Christine M: Weaving the Sermon. Preaching in a Feminist Perspektive, Louisville 1989.
- Taylor, Barbara B: The Preaching Life. Boston/Cambridge 1993.

VII. Reading and telling stories in preaching/Narrative Theory

- Alter, Robert: The Art of Biblical Narrative, New York 1981.
- Egli, Andreas: Erzählen in der Predigt. Untersuchungen zu Form und Leistungsfähigkeit erzählender Sprache in der Predigt, Zurich 1995.

- Jensen, Richard A: Thinking in Story. Preaching in a Post-literate Age, Lima 1993.
- Lowry, Eugene L: How to Preach a Parable. Designs for Narrative Sermons, Nashville 1989.
- Neidhardt, Walter e.a. (ed.): Erzählbuch zur Bibel, 1–3, 3 Vols., Lahr/Düsseldorf 1990, 1993, 1997.
- Robinson, Wayne Bradley (ed.): Journeys Toward Narrative Preaching, New York 1990.
- Steimle, Edmund/Niedenthal, Morris/Rice, Charles L: Preaching the Story, Philadelphia 1980.

VIII. Performing the Sermon

- Berger, P. L: Redeeming Laughter, Berlin/New York 1997.
- Buckner, R: The Joy of Jesus. Humour in the Gospels, Norwich 1993.
- Childers, Jana: Performing the Word. Preaching as Theatre, Nashville 1998.
- Damblon, Albert: Frei predigen. Ein Lehr- und Arbeitsbuch, Düsseldorf 1991.
- Nicol, Martin: Einander ins Bild setzen. Dramaturgische Homiletik, Göttingen 2002.
- Trueblood, D. E: Humor of Christ, New York 1964/1990
- Webb, Joseph M.: Preaching Without Notes, Nashville 2001.